w r a p s

w r a p s

easy recipes for handheld meals

mary corpening barber, sara corpening, and lori lyn narlock

photographs by frankie frankeny

CHRONICLE BOOKS

SAN FRANCISCO

Library of Congress Cataloging-in-Publication Data:
Barber, Mary Corpening, 1969–
Wraps: easy recipes for handheld meals / by Mary Corpening Barber, Sara Corpening, and Lori Lyn Narlock;
photographs by Frankie Frankeny.
p.   cm.
Includes index.
ISBN 0-8118-1812-8
1. Stuffed foods (Cookery) 2. Cookery, International.
I. Corpening, Sara, 1969–. II. Narlock, Lori Lyn, 1962–.
III. Title.
TX836.B37   1998
641.8—dc21   97-17111
                                         CIP

Manufactured in China.

Designed by Elizabeth Van Itallie
Food styling by Wesley Martin
The photographer wishes to thank Bill LeBlond and Pamela Geismar for thinking of me again,
and Lori and Mary and Sara. She also wishes to thank Fillamento in San Francisco and Vanderbilt and Company
in St. Helena, California, for the use of their beautiful tableware for the photographs.

Distributed in Canada by Raincoast Books
9050 Shaughnessy Street
Vancouver, British Columbia V6P 6E5

15 14 13 12 11 10
Chronicle Books LLC
85 Second Street
San Francisco, California 94105

www.chroniclebooks.com

i salute my little brother, ronnie,
whose memory inspires me every day
and who sparked my interest in this subject years ago
with his profound love of great food wrapped in a tortilla. —LORI

acknowledgments

from mary and sara

Mom and Dad, thank you for exposing us to so many extraordinary foods by giving us the opportunity to travel and to explore new experiences. Your influence and encouragement have been the compelling force behind this compilation of international recipes. Jack and Erik, we owe you our deepest gratitude for your patience, hearty appetites, and helpful ideas and critiques. We love you all.

from all of us

We would like to thank Andrea Cardoso; without her help we would not have been able to complete this book.

We also want to express our appreciation to Bill LeBlond, Leslie Jonath, Sarah Putman, and Pamela Geismar at Chronicle Books; they have received our phone calls, questions, and queries graciously day in and day out.

We are indebted to our friends who have spent time and effort testing recipes and offering valuable feedback, especially Fairley Pilaro, Jan Janek, Victoria Reid, Dan and Debbie Fuchs, and Lisa Schwartz.

table of contents

PB&G, RECIPE PAGE 28

what wraps are all about

Wraps are not the ballet, the symphony, or a quiet library. They are a tied basketball game with two minutes on the clock, a toe-tapping rhythm and blues show, a vibrant and colorful fireworks display for the palate. Wraps are an opportunity to sample an array of cuisines with little effort or skill. And best of all, they are also a shameless solution to the age-old dilemma of trying to pile a little bit of all things onto your fork or mash together everything on your plate without being caught by the manners police.

The song "Wrap It Up, I'll Take It" by the Fabulous Thunderbirds is the war cry of '90s cuisine and embodies one of the most basic concepts of a wrap. As the song goes, I'll take it. Maybe I'll take a wrap with me for breakfast on the go, or maybe I'll eat it for lunch at my desk. Perhaps I'll just stand over the sink and eat my wrap until I'm so stuffed I can't eat any more. Because that is what a good wrap inspires: gluttony. But not just any gluttony—this is soul-satisfying, finger-licking, just-can't-get-enough, good tastin' gratification.

What's the difference between a wrap and a burrito? The burrito was invented in Northern Mexico as a convenient way for cowboys and farmers to pack a lunch. For years, Americans have eaten burritos filled with Mexican-inspired ingredients—beans, rice, salsa, and the like. Recently, burritos took a turn to include fillings inspired by a multitude of cuisines and gained a new moniker: wrap. People are discovering that good taste knows no borders. Whether you call it a wrap, a gourmet burrito, or a brick, it's a handheld meal that explodes with flavor in each bite.

Wrapped foods are not new. Every type of cuisine includes a signature wrapped food, from Chinese egg rolls to

Greek gyros. What makes a wrap unique is that many of those same fillings and more are enclosed in a tortilla. We like tortillas because they are more user-friendly than most other wrappers and are available in sizes large enough to hold an entire meal. In this book you'll find a variety of cuisines enclosed in tortillas, everything from an all-American sloppy joe wrap to a new version of a Vietnamese spring roll.

This collection of international recipes offers both the accomplished chef and the novice cook a chance to expand their culinary repertoire and create an exciting meal without a huge investment of time or money. All of the recipes can be prepared in less than one hour and most take less than thirty minutes from start to finish. Only basic kitchen utensils and equipment are needed. The simple-to-follow techniques allow anyone to master a new dish or try a novel approach to an old favorite.

Wraps can be enjoyed morning, noon, and night. In *Eye Openers* you'll find traditional breakfast combinations to help you start your day with a smile. *Midday Satisfaction* wraps are designed to fill you up without weighing you down. *Evening Repast* recipes invite you to devour your favorite food without hesitation or remorse. *Sweet Tooth Gratification* transcends the average dessert category and goes directly to an indefinable place where engaging fillings and sumptuous wraps cannot be measured in mere mortal terms.

Whether you go forward or backward through this book, you'll find that each recipe tastes better than the last one you made. So, start wrapping up some new dishes as well as old favorites, and soon you'll be enjoying culinary masterpieces that you can eat with your fingers!

ingredients

Shopping for ingredients is the first step toward cooking a fabulous meal. It is important to make educated decisions because carefully selected ingredients will contribute to a better end result.

read the package

Remember when you were learning to read and everything that contained letters was fascinating, including the cereal box that your mother set in front of you in the morning? The ingredient description probably didn't mean anything to you then, but now it can mean the difference between an average-tasting food and a great-tasting dish. It is a good practice to read the labels of your favorite brands and compare them with their competitors. Compare the nutritional information, the fat content, and the list of chemicals and additives, if any. Avoid foods with chemical preservatives if there is a product available without these potentially harmful ingredients.

Read labels carefully, especially the nutritional data. Many products list the nutritional values for a very small and/or uncooked portion. Consider this information when you determine how this ingredient will be prepared and in what quantity. One example is that some brands of tortilla may appear to be higher in calories and fat than others, but tortilla weight varies among competing brands. A tortilla that weighs less will most likely be lower in calories and fat, but when compared to a brand that weighs more, the fat and calories may be the same ounce for ounce.

compare taste

The best way to discover a product that will become a staple in your pantry is to taste as many brands as you can. After you read the package of a ready-made item, take it home and sample it next to a brand you may already have, or buy a couple of brands of the same item and select the one you like best. This idea of taste-testing may seem time-consuming and frivolous, but there is nothing worse than preparing an entire recipe using high-quality ingredients only to find the dish is spoiled by one item that is substandard. It's a little like pouring sour milk into a cup of fresh-brewed coffee.

For nearly every ready-made ingredient included in a recipe, we have included a description and in some cases we have recommended brands we like best. Your tastes may differ and you may want to select a particular item that is sweeter, less sweet, spicier, or less spicy.

product availability

Supermarket shelves now commonly include items that not long ago were hard to find. Products such as hot and spicy sesame-soy sauces, marinades of roasted chiles, and curry pastes that were once limited to gourmet shops or specialized ethnic markets are turning up on the shelves of neighborhood grocery stores.

Large chain supermarkets are often the last to carry a locally made brand or international product; independent grocery stores often carry a wider variety of innovative products. Lesser-known products and brands are easily accessed through mail order or Internet purchasing. For ingredients or brands that may be difficult to find, see the list of manufacturers in the resource guide, page 104.

a few of our favorite things

The recipes in this book have been developed to encourage you to try new cuisines. A couple of the ingredients may be unfamiliar to you. These descriptions should dispel any mystery surrounding these delicious foods.

BACON DRIPPINGS Bacon drippings stored in an old coffee can used to be a staple in the larder. Now only grandmothers seem to have them on hand, but they are a culinary treasure that needs to be resurrected. They enhance the flavor of all foods that are cooked in them, from eggs to vegetables. Use them sparingly; a little bit will impart a lot of flavor.

Bacon drippings are easy to keep on hand. Once bacon has been cooked and removed from the pan, let the drippings cool, then pour them into a sturdy, sealable container. (A 1-ounce strip of bacon yields approximately 2 teaspoons of drippings.) Refrigerate until ready to use.

BARBECUE SAUCE This single item can make or break a recipe because flavors range from very smoky to very sweet. When purchasing a barbecue sauce, be sure to read the ingredients listed on the label and be wary of those containing a large quantity of artificial flavorings or corn syrup. Most grocery stores carry a good selection of barbecue sauces. For the best luck in finding a lip-smackin' sauce, try brands made by local producers or well-known barbecue restaurants. We like brands that are a well-rounded blend of sweet, spice, and acid.

BEANS We like to use a variety of beans in wraps for flavor variation and as a nutritious filler. Beans make the perfect substitute for meat and other protein-rich foods. We prefer the taste of home-cooked beans. However, dried beans require soaking before cooking for one to eight hours, depending on the method you use. So, for convenience, we recommend canned beans in wraps. Canned beans are cooked before being packaged and are ready to eat. They are available in a wide assortment of types.

CITRUS OILS These are brilliant oils extracted from lemons, limes, and oranges. We like to use them in recipes that traditionally use the zest of a fruit. They add spirit to all types of food, from salad dressings to fruit tarts. The brand that we prefer is called Boyajian. Citrus oils are available in gourmet stores and some supermarkets. Use them sparingly; they are very concentrated. Also, be aware of different types when buying a citrus oil: There are pure oils, which we recommend for their intense flavor, and infused oils, which have a more diluted taste.

COCONUT MILK Canned coconut milk is not actually milk from a coconut; its made from a mixture of water and fresh coconut meat that is boiled and then strained. Canned coconut milk is high in both calories and fat. Light coconut milk, which contains 60 percent less fat, is a good alternative. There is little difference between brands, but avoid sweetened varieties whenever possible. Look for coconut milk in the Asian foods section of supermarkets.

GRAINS AND PASTAS Grains are an important ingredient in wraps. They contribute to bulk and nutritional quality. Rice is primarily used in the recipes in this book, but couscous, orzo, and egg noodles are also used for variety.
 • *Couscous* is a poseur in the world of grains. Because of its shape and size it is often thought to be a grain, but it is actually a tiny pasta made from semolina flour and water. It has a mild flavor that adopts the taste of the food with which it is paired and it contributes a unique, delicate texture. It is a great substitute for any grain because it can be prepared in under ten minutes.
 • *Orzo* is often confused with rice because of its shape. It is a pasta made from wheat flours and water. It has a soft texture and is insipid on its own. Be careful not to overcook orzo or it will be mushy.
 • *Egg noodles* are short, flat noodles usually made from semolina flour, water, and eggs. They have a subtle taste that is nicely complemented by a variety of sauces.

Couscous and pastas are available in packages in the pasta section of supermarkets and in bulk in many supermarkets and natural foods stores.

GREENS These barely need mentioning, except to say *be kind to yourself.* When you set out to purchase spinach or other greens, choose the prewashed bags of greens or the loose baby leaves for the quickest and easiest preparation. These ready-to-go greens may cost a little more, but what you save in time and effort is worth the price.

HERBES DE PROVENCE Enjoy a taste of the South of France when you add this collection of dried herbs to your food. Herbes de Provence usually includes a combination of basil, thyme, fennel, sage, rosemary, and lavender. This irreplaceable blend of herbs is sold in the seasonings section of supermarkets, and natural food stores often carry it in bulk. It can be more expensive than some herb blends, but it is worth it.

HOISIN SAUCE This savory sauce has a slightly smoky-sweet taste. It is a well-balanced blend of ingredients that include garlic, peppers, and spices. It is used in many types of Chinese cuisine as a cooking and dipping sauce. It is usually available in the Asian foods section in supermarkets.

KOSHER SALT Kosher salt is retrieved from the same sources as table salt—from mines or evaporated water deposits. Unlike table salt, it is additive-free, less refined, and coarse. Because of its larger grains, the quantity may seem larger than what you're accustomed to if you are used to using table salt. If you substitute table salt for the kosher salt in these recipes, use a smaller amount. A good rule of thumb is to reduce the amount of salt by half, or ½ teaspoon of table salt for every teaspoon of kosher salt.

PICANTE SAUCE Picante sauce is an all-purpose, tomato-based sauce that is enhanced by finely chopped vegetables. It is usually thinner than salsa and the flavor is concentrated in the tomato sauce. It is made with different heat levels. Select a version that appeals to your palate and your heat tolerance. Picante sauce is sold in cans and jars in the Mexican foods section of supermarkets.

RICE This common grain is available in many varieties. Flavor, texture, and preparation time vary from one type to another, but there is no significant difference in cooking methods or nutritional values.

- *White rice* is the most commonly used rice in our wrap recipes. It is milled to produce shiny white grains in three lengths: short, medium, and long. Long grain rice, which is typically enriched with vitamins and minerals, is the most popular by far. Because of its nondescript taste it is best when used as a carrier, such as a bed for a stir-fry, or to absorb the spiciness of a food it accompanies. Medium and short grain rice are less milled and therefore have a higher starch content and are stickier when cooked. Some medium grain rice has corn syrup added to give the grains a nice sheen. Long and medium grain rice is usually available in most supermarkets, in packages and in bulk. Short grain rice can be found in supermarkets or Asian specialty markets.

- *Brown rice* is milled only to remove the husks. The wheat germ layer is left intact, resulting in a nuttier taste and higher fiber content than white rice. Wild rice and brown rice have a denser texture and take longer to cook than other rice.

- *Basmati rice* traces its origins to the foothills of the Himalayan mountains in Northern India. It is longer than long grain white rice and has an herbal essence that is detectable in its aroma and taste. U.S. farmers have cultivated a domestic version which is grown primarily in Texas.

- *Jasmine rice* grows in the wetlands of Thailand. When cooked it resembles long grain white rice. It has a distinctive floral aroma and taste.

- *Wild rice* is actually a grass seed that is grown in large quantities in the Midwest.

RICE WINE VINEGAR Distilled from rice and then fermented, rice wine vinegar has a delicious, mild flavor. It enhances many dishes, from salad dressings to dips. It is available plain or seasoned, which contains sugar and salt. Many supermarkets carry rice wine vinegar in the vinegar section.

TORTILLAS The most essential ingredient in a wrap is the edible container that holds the filling. Every recipe in this book can be prepared with a flour tortilla. Flour-based tortillas, which primarily consist of all-purpose flour, water, shortening, and leavening agents, are delicious, sturdy, and pliable, making them ideal for wrapping—unlike corn tortillas and other types of flat breads which can break when folded. Flavored flour tortillas have begun to proliferate in both savory and sweet versions, but are not available in all areas. Flavored tortillas are produced by the addition of vegetable and fruit powders as well as fresh ingredients such as chiles and herbs. If flavored tortillas are available where you shop, use the flavors we suggest, or feel free to experiment with different flavors. Always warm them to bring out the taste.

We strongly suggest purchasing tortillas that do not contain artificial preservatives, which allow for a longer shelf life, or dough conditioners, which provide elasticity. The shelf life of fresh tortillas can be lengthened by storing an opened or new package in a sealed bag in the refrigerator or freezer.

Tortilla size varies from one brand to another and from one flavor to the next. For the savory recipes, we suggest using 10- or 11-inch tortillas whenever possible, and for the sweet recipes, we use an 8-inch tortilla. If smaller tortillas are all that is available where you shop, do not overfill your wrap; increase the number of tortillas to satisfy your appetite, dividing the filling evenly among them.

wrap method

measuring

Meat and fish are measured by weight in this book. All other ingredients are measured by volume using cup and spoon sizes. When appropriate, an approximate weight or size description has been included. If there are leftovers, seal them in an airtight container and save them for later use.

chopping, dicing, and mincing

Always use a sharp knife when cutting. To chop is to cut an item into multiple pieces of a similar size. To dice is to cut an item into symmetrical, uniform pieces—usually in a cube shape. Dicing is important with ingredients that are going to be cooked because it helps ensure even doneness. In this book, mincing is used for garlic. We recommend a coarse mince to prevent garlic from burning during cooking.

seasoning with salt

We know a cook who added salt to her coffee grounds. And we know others who refuse to add even one grain of salt to their food because of a fear of sodium. Both of these are extremes. Salt is an essential ingredient because it adds dimension and brings out the flavor of food. It is important to use an amount that will result in maximum flavor. We use kosher salt and highly recommend that you use it also. If you prefer not to use kosher salt, substitute table salt, using ½ teaspoon table salt for every 1 teaspoon kosher salt.

preparing rice

Every recipe that includes rice requires warm cooked rice. The most convenient method for having warm rice on hand is to use an electric rice cooker. If you use the conventional saucepan method, always check the cooking time of the rice before beginning the recipe to ensure perfect timing.

When cooking rice in a saucepan or pot, be sure to use one large enough to hold the rice in a shallow layer. When too much rice is cooked in a small pot, it tends to clump together. For the best results, cook each type of rice according to the package directions.

For the sake of convenience, rice can be prepared ahead and reheated when needed. To do this, place cooked rice in a nonstick skillet or saucepan large enough to hold it in a shallow layer. Sprinkle the rice with a couple of tablespoons of water until moist. Cover with a lid and cook on low heat until rice is hot, 5 to 10 minutes. Or, place rice in a microwaveable container and cook on high heat for 1 to 2 minutes; stir, check heat, and continue to cook until hot.

wrapping

With practice comes perfection. The first few times you wrap the tortilla around the filling may feel a little like squeezing into pants that are a size too small. But don't worry—after a few attempts, you'll get the hang of it.

The first step to wrapping is warming the tortilla to loosen the oils so that it doesn't tear. Extremely fresh tortillas that have a generous fat content are quite pliable, but even these tortillas can easily crack or tear when being folded. Warming a tortilla can be accomplished using a variety of methods. If you have an electric stove,

place the tortilla in a large nonstick skillet over medium-high heat, cook until warm, about 15 seconds. Flip the tortilla to warm other side, about 15 seconds. If you have a gas range, turn a burner on low flame and carefully drag the tortilla back and forth across the flame a few times until it is warm. Tortillas can also be heated in a microwave oven on high heat for 10 to 15 seconds, or wrapped in aluminum foil and heated in the oven at 350°F for 3 to 5 minutes.

When the tortilla is warm, spread the filling in a 2-by-5-inch rectangle on the bottom half of the tortilla. Fold the right and left edges of the tortilla over the filling, toward the center. Fold the bottom edge of the tortilla toward the center and gently roll until the tortilla is completely wrapped around the filling. For an open-end roll, follow the same process but begin by folding the bottom edge first and then roll the wrap from one side to the other, leaving the top open.

All of the savory wraps are designed to hold 1¼ cups of filling; any more and they will tear or overflow. The sweet wraps should contain ½ cup of filling. Do not overfill a tortilla.

storing wraps

The beauty of wraps is that most can be made ahead and eaten later. Unless the recipe indicates that you should eat the wrap immediately, it can be covered in plastic wrap and stored in the refrigerator for up to 4 hours. Wraps that do not contain eggs, fish, or greens can be covered in plastic wrap and refrigerated for up to 24 hours or frozen for up to 1 week.

To heat a refrigerated wrap, cook in a microwave oven on high power for 1 to 2 minutes. Check after 1 minute by cutting it in half and testing the temperature of the center. Or, uncover the wrap and bake on a small baking sheet in the oven at 350°F for 15 to 20 minutes. Use the same process to check the temperature after 15 minutes. If the wraps are frozen, cook in a microwave oven on high power for 5 to 7 minutes, checking after 5 minutes. Or, bake on a small baking sheet in the oven at 350°F for 45 to 50 minutes. Reheating in a microwave oven will result in a softer wrap; a conventional oven will produce a crispy exterior.

equipment *checklist*

Wraps can be prepared using a minimum amount of very basic equipment and utensils. If you have the following, you are ready to cook any wrap in this book.

- BAKING DISH, 13-BY-9-BY-2-INCH
- BAKING SHEET
- CAN OPENER
- CHEESE GRATER
- CHEF'S KNIFE, 8- OR 10-INCH
- CUTTING BOARD
- LARGE NONSTICK SKILLET
- MEASURING CUPS
- MEASURING SPOONS
- MIXING BOWLS (SMALL, MEDIUM, AND LARGE)
- NONREACTIVE SKILLET (STAINLESS STEEL), RECOMMENDED FOR RECIPES THAT INCLUDE AN ACID TO PREVENT A CHEMICAL REACTION FROM OCCURRING, SUCH AS A CHANGE IN COLOR OR TASTE
- OVENPROOF GLASS BOWL OR BAKING DISH
- PARING KNIFE

- PLASTIC SPATULA
- SAUCEPANS WITH CORRESPONDING LIDS (MEDIUM AND LARGE)
- SLOTTED SPOON
- STRAINER OR COLANDER
- VEGETABLE PEELER
- WHISK OR LARGE FORK
- WOODEN SPOON

GREAT TO HAVE (BUT DON'T SWEAT IT IF YOU DON'T):
- DOUBLE BOILER
- ELECTRIC RICE COOKER

23

Breakfast is the most important meal of the day. You've heard it a million times, and it's true. But when breakfast is wrapped up in a tortilla, it takes on a magnitude of importance that your mother only dreams of. *Huevos Wrapcheros*, a combination of refried beans, scrambled eggs, and cheese, is a start to your day that you can really sink your teeth into.

PB&G, made from a mixture of peanut butter, bananas, and granola, will make you feel like a kid, putting you in a playful mood. And no matter what side of the bed you woke up on, if you indulge in the luxury of the cream cheese, gravlax, and crunchy vegetables in *This Lox Rocks*, your mood will take a swing toward true happiness.

barbecued
and sunny-side up

Now you can forget about the arduous task of soaking up the egg yolk by scraping your plate with toast. This wrap ingeniously does it for you. Just fill the tortilla with the savory ingredients and when you lift it to your mouth for the first bite, the yolk should break, spreading its delectable flavor throughout the entire wrap.

1 tablespoon plus 2 teaspoons bacon drippings or
    vegetable oil

2 cups peeled and diced potato (½-inch dice)

½ cup thinly sliced yellow onion

Kosher salt (if using table salt, decrease the amount
    by half; see page 16)

Pepper

½ cup barbecue sauce

¼ cup thinly sliced green onion, green part only

1 teaspoon dried oregano

2 eggs

Two 10- or 11-inch flour tortillas

Flavored tortilla suggestion: chipotle, tomato

Heat 1 tablespoon of the bacon drippings over medium heat in a nonstick skillet large enough to hold all of the potatoes in a single layer. Add the potatoes and yellow onion. Season with ½ teaspoon kosher salt and ¼ teaspoon pepper. Cook until crispy on all sides, 8 to 10 minutes, stirring frequently. Reduce heat and cook until tender when pierced with a fork, 5 to 10 minutes. Remove from heat.

    Transfer the potatoes to a small mixing bowl; add the barbecue sauce, green onion, and oregano. Stir to coat.

    Return the skillet to the stove, add the remaining 2 teaspoons bacon drippings, and heat over medium heat. Crack the eggs into the center of the skillet and season with ¼ teaspoon kosher salt and ¼ teaspoon pepper. Cook over high heat for 1 to 2 minutes. Remove from heat.

    Divide the potatoes evenly among the tortillas. Gently place 1 egg over potatoes, sunny-side up, and wrap (page 20). Enjoy this wrap immediately.

Serves 2

pb&g

A great alternative to a bowl of cereal, this unbeatable combination of granola, peanut butter, and bananas assembles quickly for an effortless breakfast. Enjoy it with a fruit smoothie for a nutritious start to your day.

¼ **cup peanut butter**
Two 10- or 11-inch flour tortillas
1½ **cups sliced banana (¼-inch-thick slices)**
1 cup granola

¼ **cup vanilla yogurt**
2 teaspoons honey
Flavored tortilla suggestion: **apple cinnamon,**
whole wheat

Divide the peanut butter among the tortillas and spread evenly over each tortilla, leaving at least a 1-inch border around the edge.

Combine the bananas, granola, yogurt, and honey in a small bowl. Divide the banana mixture evenly among the tortillas and wrap (page 20). Enjoy this wrap immediately.

Serves 2

apple jack

Spiced oatmeal and sweet baked apples were once declared a special occasion in Mary and Sara's household. Now we enjoy these cherished foods at whim, and you can too with this simple recipe.

2 cups peeled, cored, and diced tart green apples
  ($\frac{1}{2}$-inch dice)
$\frac{1}{4}$ cup raisins
$\frac{1}{4}$ cup honey
1 teaspoon ground cinnamon
Kosher salt (if using table salt, decrease the amount
  by half; see page 16)

1 tablespoon butter
$1\frac{1}{3}$ cups whole milk
1 cup old-fashioned oatmeal (not instant)
1 teaspoon vanilla extract
$\frac{1}{4}$ cup apple butter
Two 10- or 11-inch flour tortillas
***Flavored tortilla suggestion:* apple cinnamon**

Combine the apples, raisins, honey, cinnamon and $\frac{1}{4}$ teaspoon kosher salt in a medium bowl. Toss well to coat apples evenly.

Melt the butter in a large nonstick skillet over medium heat. Add the apples and cook until the apples feel tender when pierced with a fork, 8 to 10 minutes. Stir in the milk. Gradually stir in the oatmeal. Reduce heat to low and cook until all of the liquid has been absorbed by the oatmeal, 5 to 7 minutes. Remove from heat and add the vanilla.

Divide the apple butter among the tortillas and spread evenly over each tortilla, leaving at least a 1-inch border around the edge. Divide the apple-oatmeal mixture among the tortillas and wrap (page 20).

Serves 2

apple butter

(There is no butter in apple butter, just apples and spices. Sometimes a liquid is used in the cooking process, such as water or fruit juice. The cooked apples are puréed, strained, and canned. Purchase brands made by local farmers or those that have a lower sugar content, if possible. Apple butters are usually available near jam or applesauce in supermarkets.)

this lox
rocks

This dish is designed to combat the maddening frustration of bellying up to a platter of gravlax and trying to politely build a little sandwich of salmon, red onions, capers, and lemon juice, only to lift it to your mouth as it falls down the front of your party duds. This is great for brunch and equally good for lunch.

½ cup cream cheese, softened

2 tablespoons capers, drained and slightly chopped

1 tablespoon prepared horseradish

Pepper

Two 10- or 11-inch flour tortillas

1 cup (about 6 ounces) gravlax or smoked salmon, cut into thin strips

⅔ cup peeled and chopped cucumber

½ cup chopped fresh fennel

¼ cup chopped fresh dill

2 tablespoons chopped red onion

2 teaspoons extra virgin olive oil

Flavored tortilla suggestion: garden vegetable, spinach

Combine the cream cheese, capers, horseradish, and ⅛ teaspoon pepper in a small bowl. Divide among the tortillas and spread evenly over each tortilla, leaving at least a 1-inch border around the edge.

Mix together the remaining ingredients in a medium bowl. Divide the salmon mixture among the tortillas and wrap (page 20).

Serves 2

gravlax

(GRAVLAX is salmon that is cured in a mixture of vodka or another spirit, kosher salt, sugar, and herbs. The curing imparts the flavor of the herbs without overwhelming the taste of the fish. Gravlax is a delicacy to be enjoyed on its own or used in recipes in the same ways smoked salmon is used. Fish markets and specialty shops that sell smoked salmon usually carry gravlax, or ambitious cooks can cure their own.)

shirr
wrapsody

Traditionally, shirred eggs are whole eggs baked in individual ramekins until the whites are cooked and the yolks still tender. This recipe uses scrambled eggs combined with aromatic pesto and robust salami. It is baked in one baking dish, making assembly and cleanup easy.

4 cups water
Kosher salt (if using table salt, decrease the amount
   by half; see page 16)
1 cup cut asparagus (1-inch lengths)
4 ounces sliced salami, cut into quarters
5 eggs

¼ cup pesto
Pepper
Vegetable-oil cooking spray for coating baking dish
Two 10- or 11-inch flour tortillas
Flavored tortilla suggestion: spinach

Preheat oven to 325°F.

   Combine the water and 1 teaspoon kosher salt in a medium saucepan and bring to a boil over high heat. Add the asparagus and cook until the asparagus turns bright green and is tender yet crisp, about 1 minute. Drain the water and rinse the asparagus under cold water. Let drain completely and set aside.

   Crack the eggs into a small bowl. Whisk in the pesto, ½ teaspoon kosher salt, and ¼ teaspoon pepper. When the mixture is thoroughly combined, stir in the asparagus.

   Spray an ovenproof 6-cup glass bowl with a light coat of vegetable-oil cooking spray. Pour the egg mixture into the bowl and cover with aluminum foil. Place in preheated oven and bake for 15 minutes, remove and stir. Return to the oven and cook for 10 minutes. Do not overcook. Although the eggs may look slightly undercooked at 25 minutes, remove them from the oven and let sit a few minutes. The residual heat will finish the cooking process.

   Divide the eggs evenly among the tortillas and wrap (page 20). Enjoy this wrap immediately.

Serves 2

pesto

PESTO traditionally consists of puréed basil, olive oil, Parmesan cheese, pine nuts, and garlic. The best store-bought pesto is usually found in the refrigerator section of supermarkets. These are most likely fresh products free of artificial preservatives. We like Monterey Pasta brand because of its high-quality ingredients and the not overwhelming garlic content. Pesto has a shelf life of several weeks in the refrigerator and can be frozen for up to six months.

huevos
wrapcheros

This is our rendition of the infamous huevos rancheros, with a literal twist.

1 cup refried beans
½ cup picante sauce
3 tablespoons chopped fresh cilantro
1 teaspoon dried oregano
1 teaspoon ground cumin
½ teaspoon chili powder
⅛ teaspoon ground cinnamon

½ cup grated Monterey jack cheese
Two 10- or 11-inch flour tortillas
4 eggs
Kosher salt (if using table salt, decrease the amount
   by half; see page 16)
1 teaspoon olive oil
Flavored tortilla suggestion: **black bean, salsa, tomato**

Preheat oven to 350°F. (See Note for microwave instructions.)

Combine the beans, ¼ cup of the picante sauce, the cilantro, oregano, cumin, chili powder, and cinnamon in a small bowl. Divide the bean mixture among the tortillas and spread evenly over each tortilla, leaving at least a 1-inch border around the edge. Place the tortillas on a large baking sheet and sprinkle them with the cheese. Bake until the cheese melts, 4 to 5 minutes.

Crack the eggs into a small bowl and whisk together with ¾ teaspoon kosher salt. Heat the olive oil in a large nonstick skillet over medium heat. Add the eggs and cook until they begin to become firm, about 1 minute, stirring frequently with a plastic spatula. Add the remaining ¼ cup picante sauce and continue to cook, stirring continuously, until eggs are cooked through but still soft, about 30 seconds.

Remove the tortillas from the oven. Divide the egg mixture among the tortillas and wrap (page 20). Enjoy this wrap immediately.

N O T E : A microwave oven can be used instead of a conventional oven. Once the tortillas have been prepared with the beans and cheese, place the tortillas, one at a time, on a paper towel-lined microwaveable plate and cook on high power until the cheese melts, about 1 minute.

Serves 2

trail mix

Mary's husband, Jack, ate a bagel with cream cheese for breakfast every morning until he ate his first breakfast wrap. Now he loyally begins every day with a wrap. This is one of his favorites. The tantalizing medley of sweet apricots, crunchy cereal, and creamy yogurt will make this wrap one of your favorites, too.

¼ cup chopped almonds

1 cup plain yogurt

¼ cup chopped dried apricots

¼ cup banana chips

2 teaspoons honey

1 cup Shredded Wheat cereal, broken into pieces

2 tablespoons apricot preserves

Two 10- or 11-inch flour tortillas

Preheat oven to 350°F.

Spread the almonds on a baking sheet. Bake until they become aromatic and appear shiny from the oils being released, about 10 minutes. Remove from the oven and let cool.

Combine the almonds, yogurt, apricots, banana chips, and honey; mix well. Fold in the Shredded Wheat. Divide the apricot preserves among the tortillas and spread evenly over each tortilla, leaving at least a 1-inch border around the edge. Divide the cereal mixture among the tortillas and wrap (page 20). Enjoy this wrap immediately.

Serves 2

m i d d

Whether you call it lunch or dinner, the wraps in this chapter are the solution

to the struggle between preparing a lunch that is nourishing and delicious

versus grabbing a bite for economy of time. These wraps are equally as tasty

as they are fast to pack. Salad lovers, rejoice. Whether

you've got a hankering for a *French Kiss*—greens

enhanced by tuna, olives, and green beans—or an egg-free

Caesar complemented by shrimp, you'll become a lunch wrap devotee. If

you're hungry for a little more sustenance, wrap up the delectable combi-

nation of hummus, grilled eggplant, and fresh tomatoes in *King Tut's*

Treasure, or assemble some crumbled bacon, avocado, and smoked turkey

for *Join The Club*. Sandwiches will soon be lunch lore of yesterday.

wrap *classico*

This wrap is a burrito. Filled with savory black beans, crunchy peppers, rice, and Mexican seasonings, it is the most conventional mixture. For a more authentic treat, substitute the Monterey Jack cheese with a mild flavored Mexican or Spanish cheese, such as Manchego.

One 15½-ounce can black beans, drained
½ cup chopped red bell pepper, seeds and ribs discarded
½ cup chopped yellow bell pepper, seeds and ribs discarded
¾ cup cooked long grain white rice, warm
¼ cup chopped fresh cilantro

¼ cup picante sauce
1 tablespoon hot adobo marinade
½ teaspoon ground cumin
½ cup grated Monterey Jack cheese
Two 10- or 11-inch flour tortillas
Flavored tortilla suggestion: chipotle, whole wheat

Heat the beans in a large saucepan over medium heat. Stir in the peppers, rice, cilantro, picante sauce, adobo marinade, and cumin; cook until warm, 2 to 3 minutes.

Divide the bean mixture among the tortillas, top with the cheese, and wrap (page 20).

Serves 2

hot adobo marinade

HOT ADOBO MARINADE is a blend of dried red chiles, water, salt, and sugar. It is used as a marinade or sauce that can be added to sauces, poured over prepared dishes, or used as a grilling sauce. It has a smoky-chile taste. Look for adobo marinade in grocery stores or where Hispanic products are sold. If you aren't able to find it, a canned enchilada sauce can be substituted. Enchilada sauces are thinner and less spicy but taste very similar. We recommend Las Palmas brand. It is very good and it has a medium heat version.

cottage crunch

This is a wrap within a wrap. Cottage cheese is mixed with fresh vegetables and herbs for zest and vigor and then placed inside a crisp lettuce leaf before being wrapped inside a tortilla.

½ cup diced yellow bell pepper, seeds and ribs discarded

½ cup chopped carrot

½ cup chopped tomato, seeds discarded

3 tablespoons fresh lemon juice

3 tablespoons thinly sliced green onion, green part only

3 tablespoons chopped fresh basil

2 to 3 drops lemon oil, or 1 teaspoon chopped lemon zest

¼ teaspoon onion salt

Freshly ground pepper

1 cup large curd cottage cheese

2 large butter lettuce leaves

Two 10- or 11-inch flour tortillas

Flavored tortilla suggestion: garden vegetable

Combine the bell pepper, carrot, tomato, lemon juice, green onion, basil, lemon oil, and onion salt in a medium bowl. Add pepper to taste. Gently fold cottage cheese into vegetable mixture.

   Place a lettuce leaf on each tortilla. Divide the cottage cheese mixture among the lettuce leaf–lined tortillas and wrap (page 20). Enjoy this wrap immediately.

Serves 2

junk food junkie —*not!*

A complete meal, this wrap makes a scrumptious lunch or dinner that comes together in a New York minute!

4 cups water

Kosher salt (if using table salt, decrease the amount by half; see page 16)

1 cup chopped broccoli

¾ cup chopped tomato, seeds discarded

3 tablespoons picante sauce

3 tablespoons chopped fresh basil

3 tablespoons chopped red onion

1 tablespoon balsamic vinegar

1 tablespoon fresh lime juice

½ teaspoon minced garlic

1 cup cooked brown rice, warm

¼ cup grated sharp Cheddar cheese

Two 10- or 11-inch flour tortillas

Flavored tortilla suggestion: **whole wheat**

Combine the water and 1 teaspoon kosher salt in a medium saucepan and bring to a boil over high heat. Add the broccoli and cook until the broccoli turns bright green and is tender yet crisp, about 1 minute. Drain the water and rinse the broccoli under cold water. Let drain completely and set aside.

   Combine the tomato, picante sauce, basil, onion, vinegar, lime juice, garlic, and ¼ teaspoon kosher salt in a large bowl. Add the broccoli, rice, and cheese and stir to combine. Divide among the tortillas and wrap (page 20). Enjoy this wrap immediately.

Serves 2

king tut's
treasure

The Fertile Crescent of the Middle East is renowned for its use of hummus, a savory garbanzo bean purée. This area has historically used flatbreads and pita pockets as an edible container for dishes that use hummus as a spread. We've slathered it on a tortilla and enhanced it with grilled eggplant, fresh spinach, and tomatoes.

1 tablespoon olive oil

3 cups firmly packed cubed eggplant (½-inch cubes)

Kosher salt (if using table salt, decrease the amount by half; see page 16)

Pepper

3 teaspoons fresh lemon juice

2 teaspoons balsamic vinegar

1 cup firmly packed chopped spinach leaves

½ cup chopped tomato, seeds discarded

1 cup hummus

Two 10- or 11-inch flour tortillas

Flavored tortilla suggestion: spinach, tomato

Heat the olive oil in a large nonstick skillet over high heat until almost smoking. Add the eggplant and season with ½ teaspoon kosher salt and ¼ teaspoon pepper. Stir frequently to ensure even cooking. Cook until flesh becomes translucent, about 5 minutes, turning to brown all sides. Remove from heat and toss with 2 teaspoons of the lemon juice and the vinegar.

Toss the spinach with the tomatoes in a large bowl. Add ¼ teaspoon kosher salt, ⅛ teaspoon pepper, and the remaining 1 teaspoon lemon juice. Add the eggplant and toss.

Spread the hummus evenly over the tortillas, leaving at least a 1-inch border around the edge. Divide the eggplant mixture among the tortillas and wrap (page 20).

Serves 2

hummus

(HUMMUS is a purée of garbanzo beans (also known as chickpeas or ceci beans), ground sesame seeds, garlic, lemon juice, and olive oil. Ready-made hummus is available in supermarkets and natural food stores. If you purchase ready-made hummus, be sure to buy the freshest available. Dried hummus powder that can be mixed with water is available in packages and bulk.)

join the club

No mayo, no third piece of bread jammed in the middle, no toothpicks to eat around. Need we say more? Say goodbye to the old club and hello to this innovative replacement.

4 uncooked bacon slices, diced

½ cup chopped avocado

½ cup chopped tomato, seeds discarded

⅓ cup finely chopped red onion

2 tablespoons chopped fresh basil

1 teaspoon fresh lime juice

Kosher salt

Pepper

¼ pound thinly sliced smoked turkey

1 cup firmly packed chopped arugula

Two 10- or 11-inch flour tortillas

Flavored tortilla suggestion: tomato

Heat a large nonstick skillet over medium heat. Add bacon and cook until crispy and brown, about 5 minutes, stirring occasionally. Using a slotted spoon, transfer the bacon to a paper towel–lined plate.

Combine the avocado, tomato, onion, basil, lime juice, and bacon in a small bowl. Season with kosher salt and pepper to taste. Divide the avocado mixture evenly among the tortillas and spread over each tortilla, leaving at least a 1-inch border around the edge. Divide the turkey and arugula among the tortillas, and wrap (page 20).

Serves 2

rappin'
with a chick

Blue cheese lovers, this one's for you. The tart cherries, toasted walnuts, and roasted chicken complement and enhance the tangy taste of the blue cheese. The filling can be made ahead of time and kept refrigerated until you're ready to wrap it up.

¼ cup chopped walnuts

1 teaspoon olive oil

¾ pound boneless, skinless chicken breasts, cut into 1-inch cubes

Kosher salt (if using table salt, decrease the amount by half; see page 16)

Pepper

¼ cup firmly packed crumbled Roquefort cheese

¼ cup blue cheese dressing

⅓ cup dried cherries

¼ cup finely chopped celery

½ cup firmly packed chopped arugula

Two 10- or 11-inch flour tortillas

Flavored tortilla suggestion: spinach

Preheat oven to 350°F.

Spread the walnuts on a baking sheet. Bake until they become aromatic and appear shiny from the oils being released, about 10 minutes. Remove from the oven and let cool.

Heat the olive oil in a large nonstick skillet over high heat. Add the chicken. Season with ½ teaspoon kosher salt and ¼ teaspoon pepper. Cook until cooked through, 3 to 5 minutes, stirring to brown all sides. Let cool.

Mix together the Roquefort cheese, blue cheese dressing, cherries, and celery. Add the chicken. At this point, the filling can be refrigerated and finished later, if desired.

Toss the arugula and walnuts into the chicken mixture. Divide among the tortillas and wrap (page 20).

Serves 2

dried cherries

Riding on the coattails of dried cranberries, dried cherries are gaining popularity and offer a deep cherry flavor to all kinds of dishes, year-round. They are available in packages and in bulk in the produce department of most supermarkets.

render
unto caesar

This refreshing wrap could fill the Coliseum with fans. The eggs in the salad dressing have been replaced with citrus juices. It's a terrific complement to the shrimp and romaine lettuce.

1 tablespoon plus 2 teaspoons Dijon mustard

1 tablespoon fresh lemon juice

1 tablespoon fresh lime juice

1 teaspoon orange juice concentrate

1 teaspoon Worcestershire sauce

½ teaspoon minced garlic

Kosher salt (if using table salt, decrease the amount by half; see page 16)

3 tablespoons olive oil plus 1 teaspoon for brushing shrimp

¼ cup grated Parmesan cheese, preferably Parmigiano-Reggiano

½ pound large shrimp, peeled and deveined

Freshly ground pepper

2½ cups firmly packed chopped romaine lettuce

¼ cup croutons

Two 10- or 11-inch flour tortillas

Flavored tortilla suggestion: whole wheat

Preheat grill or broiler.

Combine the mustard, citrus juices, orange juice concentrate, Worcestershire sauce, garlic, and ¼ teaspoon kosher salt in a medium bowl. Gradually add 3 tablespoons olive oil while mixing with a whisk or a fork. Stir in the cheese. Set aside.

Brush the shrimp with the remaining 1 teaspoon olive oil and season with ¼ teaspoon kosher salt and ⅛ teaspoon pepper. Place on grill or under broiler and cook until firm and bright orange, about 2 minutes, turning once. Remove from heat and cut into quarters.

Toss together the shrimp, romaine lettuce, and croutons in a large bowl. Add the mustard mixture and toss to coat evenly. Season with salt and pepper to taste. Divide the mixture evenly among the tortillas and wrap (page 20). Enjoy this wrap immediately.

Serves 2

lulu

This unique filling is based on one of Mary and Sara's prized family recipes invented by LuLu, or Uncle Lawrence. The combination of chopped vegetables, Cheddar cheese, and seasonings makes a spicy filling. If you are in a real hurry, buy packaged shredded cheese.

3 tablespoons mayonnaise

1 tablespoon chili sauce

1 teaspoon Worcestershire sauce

1 teaspoon dry sherry

1 teaspoon chili powder

⅛ teaspoon cayenne pepper

1 cup grated sharp Cheddar cheese

½ cup chopped tomato, seeds discarded

½ cup chopped green bell pepper, seeds and ribs discarded

2 tablespoons chopped red onion

Kosher salt

Two 10- or 11-inch flour tortillas

1 cup alfalfa sprouts

Flavored tortilla suggestion: tomato

Combine the mayonnaise, chili sauce, Worcestershire sauce, sherry, chili powder, and cayenne pepper in a medium bowl. Add the cheese, tomato, bell pepper, and onion, and stir until incorporated. Season to taste with kosher salt.

Divide the cheese mixture evenly among the tortillas, top with the sprouts, and wrap (page 20). Enjoy this wrap immediately.

Serves 2

fertility special

This bundle of eggs is a devilish one—perfect for a lunch or brunch that needs a little spice. The watercress and radish add attitude.

Kosher salt (if using table salt, decrease the amount
  by half; see page 16)
4 eggs
3 tablespoons mayonnaise
1 tablespoon Dijon mustard
½ teaspoon curry powder
½ teaspoon paprika

1 cup firmly packed chopped watercress
1¼ cups chopped tomato, seeds discarded
¼ cup finely chopped radish
Pepper
Two 10- or 11-inch flour tortillas
Flavored tortilla suggestion: spinach, tomato

Fill a medium saucepan half full with hot tap water. Add 1 teaspoon kosher salt and place over medium heat. Gently place the eggs in the water and bring to a boil (starting with hot water makes it easier to peel the eggs). Reduce heat and simmer for 10 minutes. Remove the eggs from heat and plunge into cold water. When the eggs are completely cool, peel and grate them using the large grate of a handheld grater.

  Combine the mayonnaise, mustard, curry powder, and paprika in a medium bowl. Add the eggs, watercress, tomatoes, and radish. Season with kosher salt and pepper to taste.

  Divide the egg salad evenly among the tortillas and wrap (page 20). Enjoy this wrap immediately.

Serves 2

french kiss

As finicky children, Mary and Sara busied themselves at lunch removing each item from their salads until they were left with only the greens. Today, they appreciate every ingredient in this French classic and agree that it is twice as delicious wrapped up in a tortilla.

4 cups water

Kosher salt (if using table salt, decrease the amount by half; see page 16)

1 cup sliced green beans (1-inch lengths)

3 tablespoons fresh lemon juice

2 teaspoons Dijon mustard

½ teaspoon celery salt

Pepper

1 tablespoon olive oil

One 6-ounce can solid white tuna in spring water, drained

2 tablespoons pitted and chopped black olives, such as niçoise or kalamata

½ cup chopped yellow bell pepper, seeds and ribs discarded

2 tablespoons chopped red onion

2 tablespoons fresh chopped tarragon

½ cup crumbled feta cheese

Two 10- or 11-inch flour tortillas

Flavored tortilla suggestion: garden vegetable

Combine the water and 1 teaspoon kosher salt in a medium saucepan and bring to a boil over high heat. Add the green beans and cook until the green beans turn bright green and are tender yet crisp, 2 to 3 minutes. Drain the water and rinse the beans under cold water. Let drain completely and set aside.

Combine the lemon juice, mustard, celery salt, and ⅛ teaspoon pepper in a small bowl, using a whisk or a fork. Gradually add the olive oil, continuing to whisk until fully incorporated.

Combine the green beans, tuna, olives, bell pepper, onion, and tarragon in a medium bowl. Pour the vinaigrette over the salad mixture and gently toss to coat the vegetables.

Sprinkle the cheese over the tortillas and gently press into a circle in the center of the tortilla, leaving at least a 1-inch border around the edge. Divide the salad evenly among the tortillas and wrap (page 20). Enjoy this wrap immediately.

Serves 2

evening

Get away from the stove, get away from the stove, get away from the stove.

Heed this warning or you will be tempted to eat your wrap before it hits your

plate. These exquisite models of culinary genius deserve to be relished while

sitting down with a glass of wine, a bottle of beer, or an icy-cold cup of

milk. This collection of wraps takes you all the way around the world and

back home again to your own backyard. *Thai One On*'s aromatic blend

of curry and lemongrass added to chicken and jasmine rice gives you a taste of the Far East. Capture the Wild West on your barbecue grill with *Rodeo Roundup*, a combination of Texas-style barbecued beef and savory mashed potatoes. The nostalgic taste of mom's cooking is easily identified in *Sloppy Joe*, a slightly piquant blend of ground beef and sausage with a tomato sauce.

past

king creole

In New Orleans, nothing is sacred except food. This specialty of the South's culinary mecca is traditionally served for dinner on Monday nights, but you can enjoy it every night of the week.

1 tablespoon olive oil
1 cup diced onion
1 cup diced celery
1 tablespoon dried oregano
1 tablespoon paprika
2 teaspoons onion powder
2 bay leaves

Kosher salt (if using table salt, decrease the amount by half; see page 16)
One 15½-ounce can kidney beans, including liquid
1 pound andouille sausage, cut into ¼-inch-thick slices
1 cup cooked long grain white rice, warm
Four 10- or 11-inch flour tortillas
Flavored tortilla suggestion: black bean, tomato

Heat the olive oil in a large nonstick skillet over medium heat. Add the onion, celery, oregano, paprika, onion powder, and bay leaves. Cook until onions become tender, about 5 minutes. Season with ½ teaspoon kosher salt. Transfer to a large saucepan and add the beans. Heat over medium heat.

Clean the skillet thoroughly to remove all of the spice residue. Return the skillet to the stove and heat over high heat. Add the sausage and cook until crisp, about 5 minutes, turning to brown all sides.

Transfer the sausage to the bean mixture using a slotted spoon. Add the rice and stir to combine. Remove the bay leaves, divide the filling among the tortillas, and wrap (page 20).

Serves 4

andouille sausage

(ANDOUILLE SAUSAGE is one of the finest contributions the French made to Cajun cooking. It is a full-flavored sausage complete with garlic and seasonings. If you can't find it, substitute kielbasa or hot links in its place.)

chow sal-mein

This beats Chinese take-out any day.

⅓ cup oyster sauce

2 tablespoons orange marmalade

2 tablespoons soy sauce

¼ teaspoon orange oil, or 2 teaspoons chopped orange zest

1 tablespoon plus 1 teaspoon grated fresh ginger

2 teaspoons cornstarch

2 tablespoons olive oil

1 tablespoon minced garlic

1 cup thinly sliced strips green bell pepper, seeds and ribs discarded

2 cups firmly packed shredded cabbage

One 8-ounce can water chestnuts, drained and sliced

1 pound salmon fillet, cut into 1-inch cubes

1 teaspoon Chinese five spice powder

Kosher salt (if using table salt, decrease the amount by half; see page 16)

Pepper

1½ cups cooked long grain white rice, warm

½ cup crunchy chow mein noodles

Four 10- or 11-inch flour tortillas

Combine the oyster sauce, marmalade, soy sauce, orange oil, ginger, and cornstarch in a small bowl.

Heat 1 tablespoon of the olive oil in a large nonstick skillet over medium heat. Add the garlic; cook 30 seconds. Add the bell pepper, cabbage, and water chestnuts. Cook until cabbage wilts, 2 to 3 minutes, stirring frequently. Add the oyster sauce mixture and stir well. Cook until sauce begins to boil, about 1 minute. Remove from heat. Transfer the vegetables to a medium bowl.

Clean the skillet thoroughly and return it to the stove. Add the remaining 1 tablespoon olive oil and heat over medium-high heat. Sprinkle the five spice powder, 1 teaspoon kosher salt, and ¼ teaspoon pepper evenly over the salmon. Add the salmon and cook until firm and cooked through, about 3 minutes, stirring to brown all sides.

Add the vegetables and rice to the salmon and stir gently to mix. Fold in the chow mein noodles. Divide among the tortillas and wrap (page 20).

Serves 4

微波炉
oyster sauce
外卖盒
chinese five-spice powder

(OYSTER SAUCE, a reduction of oysters cooked in soy sauce, is a common ingredient in many Asian dishes. CHINESE FIVE SPICE POWDER is a blend of sweet spices and savory herbs consisting of cinnamon, cloves, fennel, star anise, and Szechwan peppercorns. These ingredients are commonly available in the Asian foods section of most supermarkets.)

italian *revolution*

The pancetta has been replaced with bacon in this creamy Italian dish, a variation on carbonara. It has a creamy texture, robust flavor, and stick-to-your-ribs sustenance.

4 uncooked bacon slices, diced

1¼ pounds boneless, skinless chicken breasts,
  cut into ¼-inch-thick strips

Kosher salt (if using table salt, decrease the amount
  by half; see page 16)

Pepper

1 tablespoon olive oil

1 cup diced onion

1 teaspoon all-purpose flour

¾ cup dry white wine

½ cup heavy cream

⅛ teaspoon ground nutmeg

1 cup green peas

1 cup grated Swiss cheese

1½ cups warm cooked orzo

Four 10- or 11-inch flour tortillas

Flavored tortilla suggestion: salsa

Heat a large nonstick skillet over medium heat. Add the bacon and cook until crispy and brown, about 5 minutes, stirring occasionally. Transfer the bacon to a paper towel-lined plate using a slotted spoon.

Return the skillet to the stove and heat over high heat. Add the chicken and season with 1 teaspoon kosher salt and ¼ teaspoon pepper. Cook until chicken is cooked through, 4 to 6 minutes, turning to brown all sides. Remove from heat and transfer the chicken to a large bowl using a slotted spoon. Add the bacon and gently stir to combine.

Wipe the skillet clean with a paper towel to remove all meat residue and return the skillet to the stove. Add the olive oil and heat over medium heat. Add the onion, flour, ½ teaspoon kosher salt, and ¼ teaspoon pepper. Cook until the onions become soft, about 10 minutes. Add the wine and cream and bring to a boil. Cook until mixture becomes thick, 4 to 5 minutes. Add the nutmeg and peas; cook 1 minute. Add the chicken mixture, cheese, and orzo and stir to combine thoroughly. Divide among the tortillas and wrap (page 20).

Serves 4

down by *the sea*

Onions caramelized in lemon juice and vinegar add a unique zest to this blend of swordfish and olives, which comes straight from the Mediterranean. Feel free to substitute another firm fish, such as tuna, in place of the swordfish.

2 tablespoons plus 2 teaspoons olive oil

4 cups firmly packed thinly sliced onion

Kosher salt (if using table salt, decrease the amount
   by half; see page 16)

Pepper

⅓ cup fresh lemon juice

¼ cup Champagne vinegar

1 tablespoon dried tarragon

1¼ pounds swordfish, cut into 1-inch cubes

¼ cup pitted and chopped black olives, such as kalamata

3 cups firmly packed chopped arugula

Four 10- or 11-inch flour tortillas

Flavored tortilla suggestion: spinach

Preheat grill or broiler.

Heat 2 tablespoons of the olive oil in a large nonstick skillet over medium heat. Add the onion, ½ teaspoon kosher salt, and ¼ teaspoon pepper. Cook until onions are tender and begin to turn golden brown, about 10 minutes. Add the lemon juice, vinegar, and tarragon; cook until liquid is evaporated, about 10 minutes, stirring frequently.

Toss the swordfish with the remaining 2 teaspoons olive oil, and season with ½ teaspoon kosher salt and ¼ teaspoon pepper. Place on grill or under broiler and cook until firm, about 5 minutes, turning once. Remove from heat. Transfer the fish to a large bowl and add the onion mixture, olives, and arugula. Toss to mix well. Divide among the tortillas and wrap (page 20).

Serves 4

champagne vinegar

CHAMPAGNE VINEGAR is a mild-tasting vinegar made from champagne. It is readily available in supermarkets next to vinegars and salad dressings and can be used in place of white wine vinegar when cooking or preparing a vinaigrette.

rodeo roundup

To be fair, Mary and Sara must warn fellow North Carolinians that this is not the barbecue they know. This is a Texas-style barbecue full of beef and tomato sauce. We recommend always using fresh corn when it is available.

2 tablespoons red wine vinegar

1 tablespoon Dijon mustard

2 teaspoons minced garlic

¼ cup plus 1 teaspoon olive oil

1 pound Yukon Gold (or small white) potatoes, peeled and cut into 1-inch cubes

Kosher salt (if using table salt, decrease the amount by half; see page 16)

¼ cup milk

2 tablespoons butter, softened

2 tablespoons sour cream

2 tablespoons chopped fresh chives

Pepper

1 cup corn kernels

1¼ pounds London broil, cut into ¼-inch-thick strips

⅓ cup barbecue sauce

Four 10- or 11-inch flour tortillas

Flavored tortilla suggestion: black bean, salsa

Preheat grill or broiler. Combine the vinegar, mustard, garlic, and ¼ cup olive oil in a large bowl. Add the meat, stir to coat, and marinate for 15 minutes.

Place the potatoes and 1 tablespoon kosher salt in a large saucepan and cover with water. Bring to a boil over high heat, reduce heat, and simmer until potatoes are tender when pierced with a fork, about 20 minutes. Drain the potatoes, return to the pan, and mash, using a whisk or a large fork. Add the milk, butter, sour cream, and chives and mix well. Season with ½ teaspoon kosher salt and ¼ teaspoon pepper.

Heat the remaining 1 teaspoon olive oil in a large nonstick skillet over medium heat. Add the corn, ½ teaspoon kosher salt, and ¼ teaspoon pepper. Cook until the corn is tender, about 3 minutes. Remove from heat.

Season the beef with salt and pepper. Cook on grill or under broiler until browned but still rare inside, about 5 minutes, turning once. Transfer to skillet with corn. Add barbecue sauce and stir to combine.

Divide the potatoes among the tortillas and spread evenly over each tortilla, leaving at least a 1-inch border around the edge. Divide the meat mixture among the tortillas and wrap (page 20).

Serves 4

tofu *twister*

Meatless and marvelous sums up this savory combination of tofu, spinach, and shiitakes. The tofu is marinated and cooked in a piquant sesame-soy sauce, which is balanced by the sweet potatoes.

⅓ cup hoisin sauce

¼ cup soy sauce

1 tablespoon sesame oil

1 tablespoon grated ginger

2 teaspoons minced garlic

1 tablespoon plus 2 teaspoons olive oil

2 cups sliced shiitake mushrooms, stems removed and discarded

2 cups peeled and diced sweet potatoes (½-inch cubes)

3 cups firmly packed chopped kale

One 14-ounce package firm tofu, completely drained and cut into ½-inch cubes

1 cup cooked brown rice, warm

Four 10- or 11-inch flour tortillas

Flavored tortilla suggestion: spinach, whole wheat

Combine the hoisin sauce, soy sauce, sesame oil, grated ginger, and minced garlic in a medium bowl. Set aside.

Heat 1 tablespoon of the olive oil in a large nonstick skillet over medium-high heat. Add the mushrooms and cook until mushrooms begin to brown and become crispy, about 10 minutes. Transfer to a small bowl.

Return the skillet to the stove. Heat the remaining 2 teaspoons olive oil over medium heat. Add the sweet potatoes and cook until they become tender when pierced with a fork, about 5 minutes, stirring to brown all sides. Add the kale and sesame-soy sauce; cook until kale wilts, about 1 minute, stirring constantly. Gently fold in tofu, mushrooms, and rice. Cook until mixture is warm and liquid has been completely absorbed. Divide among the tortillas and wrap (page 20).

Serves 4

nuts for *thai food*

Peanuts are a common ingredient used in Thai cookery, from the chopped peanuts added to pad Thai to the savory peanut sauce that accompanies chicken satay. In this vegetarian recipe, a spicy peanut sauce imparts a robust flavor to the creamy tofu and crunchy vegetables.

1 tablespoon plus 2 teaspoons olive oil

2 cups diced carrot

1½ cups diced onion

2 cups diced snow peas

2 tablespoons soy sauce

One 14-ounce package firm tofu, drained completely and cut into ½-inch cubes

½ cup peanut sauce

¼ cup chopped fresh cilantro

Four 10- or 11-inch flour tortillas

Heat 1 tablespoon of the olive oil in a large nonstick skillet over medium heat. Add the carrot, onion, snow peas, and 1 tablespoon of the soy sauce and cook until vegetables are tender but still crisp, 5 to 7 minutes. Remove from heat and transfer vegetables to a medium bowl.

Wipe the skillet clean with a paper towel and return the skillet to the stove. Add the remaining 2 teaspoons olive oil and heat over medium-high heat. Add the tofu and the remaining 1 tablespoon soy sauce. Cook until tofu is heated through, about 5 minutes. Turn to cook all sides evenly. Add the vegetables to the skillet and gently stir to mix. Gently fold in the peanut sauce and cilantro. Divide the mixture among the tortillas and wrap (page 20).

Serves 4

peanut sauce

PEANUT SAUCES are available in as many styles as there are bags of peanuts sold at a Saturday afternoon baseball game in Virginia. For the best results, use a peanut sauce that is not too sweet or too thin. We prefer brands that have a hint of fire, such as Saveur or House of Tsang.

chimichurri *bang bang*

The antidote to the familiar, chimichurri is a zesty South American pesto that adds a flavorful impact to this combination of tender fish, crunchy vegetables, and sweet fruit.

1 cup chopped mango

½ cup chopped red bell pepper, seeds and ribs discarded

½ cup chopped fresh cilantro

½ cup chopped fresh parsley

¼ cup fresh lime juice

3 tablespoons white wine vinegar

1 tablespoon minced garlic

1 tablespoon dried oregano

2 teaspoons chopped fresh jalapeño, with seeds

Kosher salt (if using table salt, decrease the amount by half; see page 16)

Pepper

1 tablespoon olive oil

1 pound red snapper fillet, cut into ½-inch cubes

One 14½-ounce can black beans, drained

1 cup cooked long grain white rice, warm

Four 10- or 11-inch flour tortillas

Flavored tortilla suggestion: black bean, chipotle

Combine the mango, bell pepper, cilantro, parsley, lime juice, vinegar, garlic, oregano, and jalapeño in a medium bowl. Season with ½ teaspoon kosher salt and ¼ teaspoon pepper.

Heat the olive oil in a large nonstick skillet over medium-high heat. Add the fish; season with ½ teaspoon kosher salt and ¼ teaspoon pepper. Cook until fish becomes firm and turns white, about 5 minutes, turning to cook evenly. Add the beans and rice. Cook until beans are warm, 1 to 2 minutes. Remove from heat. Add the mango mixture; stir well. Divide among the tortillas and wrap (page 20). Enjoy this wrap immediately.

Serves 4

california
wrap

Sushi chefs beware—you may need a new career! This wrap captures the taste of one of the best-loved sushi rolls, the California roll, in an easy to eat, edible container. If you can't find short grain white rice, substitute medium grain white rice.

1 teaspoon powdered wasabi

1 teaspoon water

1 tablespoon soy sauce

2 cups cooked short grain rice, at room temperature

¼ cup seasoned rice wine vinegar

¾ pound fresh crabmeat

1 cup chopped avocado

1 cup peeled and chopped cucumber, seeds discarded

½ cup sliced green onion, green part only

¼ cup chopped pickled ginger

2 tablespoons mayonnaise

4 sheets nori

Four 10- or 11-inch flour tortillas

Flavored tortilla suggestion: spinach

Dissolve the wasabi in the water in a small bowl. Add the soy sauce. Combine this mixture with the rice in a large bowl. Add the vinegar and gently stir in the crabmeat, avocado, cucumber, green onion, ginger, and mayonnaise.

Line each tortilla with a sheet of nori. Divide the rice mixture among the nori-lined tortillas and wrap (page 20).

Serves 4

nori,
pickled ginger,
wasabi

(NORI, a dried sheet of seaweed, has a crisp, papery texture. It adds an earthy taste to all types of Japanese food, from sushi to rice dishes. PICKLED GINGER is thinly sliced ginger preserved in vinegar. It has a slightly sweet taste and is served with sushi and other Japanese dishes. WASABI is a powdered horseradish that is rather pungent, adding a peppery element to sushi. All of these ingredients can usually be found in the Asian foods section in supermarkets.)

hoppin' johnny

Black-eyed peas, the prominent ingredient in this Southern mainstay, are believed to bring good luck on New Year's Day. Eat this delicious wrap anytime for a measure toward good taste, at least, throughout the year.

One 15½-ounce can black-eyed peas, drained

2 cups cooked long grain white rice, warm

1½ cups diced tomato, seeds discarded

⅓ cup chopped fresh parsley

⅓ cup sliced green onions, white and green parts

1 teaspoon minced garlic

Kosher salt

Pepper

½ cup sour cream

1 cup grated sharp white Cheddar cheese

Four 10- or 11-inch flour tortillas

Heat the black-eyed peas in a large nonreactive saucepan over medium heat. Add the rice, tomatoes, parsley, green onions, and garlic. Season with kosher salt and pepper to taste. Cook over low heat until warm, 2 to 3 minutes. Stir to combine thoroughly.

Divide the sour cream among the tortillas and spread evenly over each tortilla, leaving at least a 1-inch border around the edge. Sprinkle the cheese evenly over the sour cream. Divide the black-eyed pea mixture among the tortillas and wrap (page 20).

Serves 4

sook and jimmy

In the Carolinas, crabbing is a common activity in the summertime. Crabbers can be found lined up along the beaches and tributaries, pulling a string with a chicken leg attached back and forth in the water, hoping to catch a sook or jimmy—the true Southerner's names for female and male crabs.

1 pound fresh spinach leaves

1 tablespoon plus 1 teaspoon olive oil

1 cup diced onion

Kosher salt (if using table salt, decrease the amount by half; see page 16)

Pepper

½ cup dry sherry

4 cups sliced white mushrooms

1 cup cream cheese, softened

¾ pound crabmeat

1½ cups cooked wild rice, warm

½ cup freshly grated Parmesan cheese

2 teaspoons fresh lemon juice

Freshly grated nutmeg

Four 10- or 11-inch flour tortillas

Flavored tortilla suggestion: spinach

Heat a large nonstick skillet over medium heat. Fill the pan with spinach leaves. (Spinach has a high water content, so no liquid is necessary for cooking.) Cook until wilted, stirring to cook evenly. Transfer to a colander. Repeat until all of the spinach is cooked, and set spinach aside.

Clean the skillet thoroughly. Put in 2 teaspoons of the olive oil and heat over medium heat. Add the onion and season with ½ teaspoon kosher salt and ¼ teaspoon pepper. Cook until onions are tender, 5 to 7 minutes. Add the sherry and cook until liquid is nearly evaporated, about 2 minutes. Transfer to a small bowl.

Wipe the skillet clean with a paper towel and return the skillet to the stove. Add the remaining 2 teaspoons olive oil and heat over medium-high heat. Add the mushrooms and season with ½ teaspoon kosher salt and ¼ teaspoon pepper. Cook until mushrooms are evenly browned, about 10 minutes. Reduce the heat to low, add the cream cheese and stir until melted, 2 to 3 minutes. Add the spinach, onions, crabmeat, rice, cheese, lemon juice, and nutmeg. Season with kosher salt and pepper, to taste.

Divide the crab mixture among the tortillas and wrap (page 20).

Serves 4

mediterranean
cachet

The saffron, fresh herbs, and scallops in this pan-Mediterranean wrap are redolent of Spanish paella. But this dish is made on the stovetop and does not require shelling any seafood.

3½ cups cold water

¾ cup uncooked long grain white rice

1 tablespoon plus 2 teaspoons extra virgin olive oil

Kosher salt (if using table salt, decrease the amount by half; see page 16)

¼ teaspoon saffron threads

⅛ teaspoon turmeric

2 cups dry white wine

2 bay leaves

1 pound bay scallops

One 6½-ounce jar artichoke hearts, drained and chopped

¾ cup roasted red bell peppers, drained and chopped

¼ cup pitted and chopped black olives, such as kalamata

1 tablespoon fresh lemon juice

1 tablespoon chopped fresh thyme

2 teaspoons chopped fresh rosemary

1 teaspoon minced garlic

Four 10- or 11-inch flour tortillas

Flavored tortilla suggestion: chipotle, tomato

Combine 1½ cups of the cold water, the rice, 2 teaspoons of the olive oil, ½ teaspoon kosher salt, the saffron, and turmeric in a medium saucepan. Bring to a boil over low heat. Simmer, covered, until all liquid is absorbed, about 20 minutes. Do not stir while rice is cooking.

Combine the remaining 2 cups water, the wine, bay leaves, and 1 teaspoon kosher salt in a medium saucepan over medium-high heat. Bring to a boil. Add the scallops and cook until scallops become opaque, about 2 minutes. Drain the liquid and return the scallops to the pan. Add the rice, artichokes, bell pepper, olives, lemon juice, thyme, rosemary, garlic, and remaining 1 tablespoon olive oil to the pan with the scallops; heat over low heat. Cook until warm, 2 to 3 minutes. Divide the scallop mixture among the tortillas and wrap (page 20).

Serves 4

vindaloo lounge

Indian cuisine relies heavily on spices that are blended together to create a distinctive dry mixture, paste, or sauce. Curry powder, garam masala, and vindaloo are a few of the common blends used in everyday dishes. This recipe uses a ready-made fiery vindaloo sauce.

1 tablespoon olive oil

¾ cup diced celery

¾ cup diced onion

Kosher salt (if using table salt, decrease the amount by half; see page 16)

2 cups cooked basmati rice, warm

One 15½-ounce can kidney beans, drained

One 15½-ounce can garbanzo beans, drained

¾ cup vindaloo sauce

Four 10- or 11-inch flour tortillas

Flavored tortilla suggestion: black bean, whole wheat

Heat the olive oil in a large nonstick skillet over medium heat. Add the celery and onion. Season with ½ teaspoon kosher salt and cook until tender, 5 to 7 minutes. Reduce heat. Add the rice, kidney and garbanzo beans, and vindaloo sauce. Mix well. Divide among the tortillas and wrap (page 20).

Serves 4

vindaloo sauce

VINDALOO SAUCE is an aromatic, robust blend of roasted chiles and spices that is used in regional Indian cooking. We are enamored by a brand called Mezban, which boasts that it is a family recipe that has been handed down for generations. Vindaloo cooking sauce is available in cans and jars in the Asian foods section in supermarkets and in Asian specialty stores.

taj mahal

Capture the best of India with this blend of curry, yogurt, and peanuts. Similar to a traditional Indian lamb stew, this wrap is further enhanced with the addition of a chutney before being wrapped to eat.

1 tablespoon plus 1 teaspoon olive oil

¾ cup chopped carrot

½ cup chopped onion

1 teaspoon curry powder

1 teaspoon ground cumin

¼ teaspoon ground cardamom

Kosher salt (if using table salt, decrease the amount by half; see page 16)

Pepper

1¼ pounds boneless lamb, cut into ¾-inch cubes

2 cups cooked basmati rice, warm

½ cup plain yogurt

½ cup mango chutney

¼ cup sliced green onions, white and green parts

¼ cup chopped peanuts

Four 10- or 11-inch flour tortillas

Flavored tortilla suggestion: chipotle, spinach

Heat 2 teaspoons of the olive oil in a large nonstick skillet over medium heat. Add the carrot, onion, curry powder, cumin, and cardamom. Season with ½ teaspoon kosher salt. Cook until onion is transparent, 3 to 5 minutes. Transfer to a small bowl.

Wipe the skillet clean and return it to the stove. Add the remaining 2 teaspoons olive oil and heat over high heat. Add the lamb and season with 1 teaspoon kosher salt and ¼ teaspoon pepper. Cook until cooked through, 3 to 5 minutes, turning to brown all sides. Add the vegetables, rice, yogurt, chutney, green onions, and peanuts. Mix well. Divide among the tortillas and wrap (page 20).

Serves 4

chutney

CHUTNEY is a sweet relish that is frequently made with mango, a native Indian fruit. But chutneys are made with many types of fruit and they range in texture from chunky to smooth, and in taste from sweet to spicy. They differ from jams and jellies because they usually have vinegar and spices that impart a savory essence. Hands down, our favorite brand is Major Grey, which has a perfect balance of sugar, heat, and acid. Chutneys are available in supermarkets in the Asian foods section or in the section where sauces, relishes, or jams are sold.

vietnamese
wrap-ease

This wrap will appeal to all of your senses. The vibrant colors of the mango, carrots, fresh mint, and basil tease your palate with a hint of what's to come: a flavorful and refreshing sensual sensation.

5 ounces maifun rice sticks

¼ cup plus 1 tablespoon seasoned rice wine vinegar

¼ cup fresh lime juice

1 tablespoon Asian-style fish sauce

½ teaspoon crushed red pepper

3 drops lime oil, or 1 teaspoon chopped fresh lime zest

1½ cups grated carrot

1 cup chopped mango

½ cup sliced green onion, white and green parts

½ cup chopped fresh basil

½ cup chopped fresh mint

2 tablespoons black sesame seeds

4 large Boston lettuce leaves, trimmed to fit in tortilla

Four 10- or 11-inch flour tortillas

Cover noodles with hot water in a large bowl; let sit 10 minutes. Drain completely; it is important to remove all excess water.

Combine the vinegar, lime juice, fish sauce, red pepper, and lime oil in a large bowl. Add the noodles and toss to coat evenly. Add the carrot, mango, green onion, basil, mint, and sesame seeds and mix well.

Place 1 lettuce leaf on each tortilla. Divide the noodle mixture among the lettuce leaf–lined tortillas and wrap (page 20). Enjoy this wrap immediately.

Serves 4

maifun rice sticks, fish sauce

MAIFUN RICE STICKS are very thin noodles made from ground rice, cornstarch, and water. They don't require cooking; they only need to be soaked before eating. Rice sticks are available in the Asian foods section of supermarkets. FISH SAUCE Don't smell the fish sauce before using it or you may be afraid to pour it into your dish. Its pungent odor comes from its composition of anchovies, salt, and water. Fish sauce can be found in specialty stores and in the Asian foods section of some supermarkets.

chicken song

Mary and Sara brought this recipe with them to San Francisco when they moved away from their favorite Chinese restaurant in New York. A scrumptious ginger sauce coats the chicken and vegetables, which are paired beautifully with the crisp lettuce lining the tortilla.

3 tablespoons soy sauce

1 tablespoon dry sherry

1 tablespoon minced garlic

1 tablespoon grated ginger

¼ teaspoon crushed red pepper

1¼ pounds boneless, skinless chicken breasts, finely chopped

2 tablespoons olive oil

1¼ cups diced celery

1¼ cups diced carrot

1¼ cups diced yellow onion

Kosher salt (if using table salt, decrease the amount by half; see page 16)

1 tablespoon cornstarch

½ cup chopped green onion, white and green parts

½ cup chopped cashew nuts

¾ cup hoisin sauce

4 large iceberg lettuce leaves, trimmed to fit inside tortilla

Four 10- or 11-inch flour tortillas

Flavored tortilla suggestion: spinach

Combine the soy sauce, sherry, garlic, ginger, and red pepper in a medium bowl. Add the chicken and toss to coat evenly. Let marinate 15 minutes.

Heat the olive oil in a large nonstick skillet over medium heat. Add the celery, carrot, and onion. Season with ½ teaspoon kosher salt and cook until the vegetables are tender, 5 to 7 minutes. Transfer to a medium bowl.

Wipe the skillet clean with a paper towel and return it to the stove. Heat the skillet over high heat. Sprinkle the chicken with cornstarch and add it to the hot skillet. Cook until the chicken is cooked through and the pan juices have thickened, 3 to 4 minutes. Add the vegetables, green onion, cashews, and hoisin sauce. Line each tortilla with a lettuce leaf. Divide the chicken mixture among the lettuce leaves and wrap (page 20). Enjoy this wrap immediately.

Serves 4

thai one on

Basil, mint, and curry paste used in combination with the coconut milk and lemongrass make this wrap distinctly Thai flavored.

1 cup light coconut milk

1 tablespoon minced fresh or preserved lemongrass, or 1 teaspoon dried lemongrass

1 tablespoon red curry paste

1 tablespoon brown sugar

Kosher salt (if using table salt, decrease the amount by half; see page 16)

1 tablespoon fresh lime juice

2 tablespoons olive oil

2 cups diced zucchini

1 cup diced onion

1¼ pounds boneless, skinless chicken breasts, cut into 1-inch cubes

2 cups cooked jasmine rice, warm

¼ cup chopped fresh basil

¼ cup chopped fresh mint

Four 10- or 11-inch flour tortillas

Flavored tortilla suggestion: chipotle, garden vegetable

Combine the coconut milk, lemongrass, curry paste, brown sugar, and 1 teaspoon kosher salt in a medium saucepan over medium heat. Bring to a simmer and cook until liquid thickens, 10 to 15 minutes. Remove from heat. Add the lime juice and set aside.

Heat 1 tablespoon of the olive oil in a large nonstick skillet over medium heat. Add the zucchini and onion, season with ½ teaspoon kosher salt, and cook until the vegetables become tender, 5 to 7 minutes. Transfer to a large bowl.

Wipe the skillet clean with a paper towel and return the skillet to the stove. Add the remaining 1 tablespoon olive oil and heat over medium heat. Add the chicken and season with 1 teaspoon kosher salt. Cook until cooked through, about 5 minutes, turning to brown all sides. Add the vegetables, rice, basil, and mix well. Stir in the coconut milk sauce. Divide the mixture among the tortillas and wrap (page 20).

Serves 4

curry paste, lemongrass

THAI, INDIAN, AND CHINESE CURRY PASTES are readily accessible today. Most are used as a base for a sauce that is cooked before being mixed with other food. Thai Kitchens makes one of our favorite red curry pastes. Look for bottled curry pastes in the Asian foods section of supermarkets. LEMONGRASS This herb is used in many Thai dishes, from soups to curries. It is available fresh in stalks in the produce department in many supermarkets. Preserved lemongrass is available in some gourmet stores and supermarkets; use it as you would fresh lemongrass. Dried lemongrass is also available and easy to use; substitute 1 teaspoon dried lemongrass for every tablespoon of fresh.

sloppy joe

Move over, hamburger buns! Sloppy Joes have been rejuvenated with the addition of spicy sausage and a tortilla to wrap the delicious, not-so-sloppy filling. Try this new approach to a longtime family favorite.

¾ cup chili sauce

3 tablespoons tomato paste

1 tablespoon Worcestershire sauce

1 tablespoon red wine vinegar

2 teaspoons dried oregano

1 teaspoon ground cumin

2 tablespoons olive oil

1 cup diced yellow onion

Kosher salt (if using table salt, decrease the amount by half; see page 16)

Pepper

¾ pound lean ground beef

½ pound spicy sausage, removed from the casing and crumbled

2 cups cooked long grain white rice, warm

½ cup thinly sliced green onion, green part only

½ cup sour cream

Four 10- or 11-inch flour tortillas

Flavored tortilla suggestion: salsa, tomato

Combine the chili sauce, tomato paste, Worcestershire sauce, and vinegar in a small bowl. Stir in the oregano and cumin and set aside.

Heat the olive oil in a large nonstick skillet over medium heat. Add the yellow onion, ½ teaspoon kosher salt, and ¼ teaspoon pepper. Cook until onions are tender, about 5 minutes. Transfer to the chili sauce mixture and stir to combine.

Return the skillet to the stove. Heat the skillet over medium heat and add the ground beef and sausage. Season with the remaining ½ teaspoon kosher salt. Cook until the meat is completely browned, 6 to 8 minutes. Add the onion mixture, rice, and green onion and mix well.

Divide the sour cream among the tortillas and spread evenly over each tortilla, leaving at least a 1-inch border around the edge. Divide the meat mixture among the tortillas and wrap (page 20).

Serves 4

what a jerk!

This is fast food from the islands, where jerk sauces and spice rubs are an everyday occurrence. In Jamaica, street vendors offer meats that are marinated in a jerk sauce and then cooked over hot charcoals. Create the atmosphere of the islands when you serve these wraps by adding a Red Stripe beer and playing a little Bob Marley in the background.

1¼ pounds boneless, skinless chicken breasts, cut into
   1-inch cubes
Kosher salt (if using table salt, decrease the amount
   by half; see page 16)
½ teaspoon ground cinnamon
¼ teaspoon allspice
⅓ cup jerk sauce (liquid version, not dry seasoning mix
   or rub)

2 cups cooked long grain white rice, warm
¾ cup diced fresh pineapple (½-inch cubes)
¼ cup chopped macadamia nuts
3 tablespoons chopped fresh mint
2 teaspoons fresh lime juice
Four 10- or 11-inch flour tortillas
Flavored tortilla suggestion: chile, spinach

Preheat oven to 400°F.

   Combine the chicken with 1 teaspoon kosher salt, cinnamon, and allspice in a medium bowl. Add the jerk sauce and toss to coat evenly.

   Spread the chicken mixture evenly into a 13-by-9-by-2-inch baking pan. Bake until chicken is cooked through, 10 to 15 minutes. Add the rice, pineapple, nuts, mint, and lime juice and mix thoroughly. Divide among the tortillas and wrap (page 20).

Serves 4

jerk sauce

(This Caribbean specialty is a fiery blend of onions, sugar, hot peppers, and vinegar. We like a brand called Busha Brownes because it is a balanced blend of sweet, spice, and acid. Jerk sauce is available in supermarkets in the hot pepper and barbecue sauce section.)

santa fe fetish

This savory chicken chili with a Southwestern flair is a cinch! Blend a batch of margaritas, invite some friends over, and serve these wraps for an effortless, fun fiesta!

1¼ pounds boneless, skinless chicken breasts, cut into
   1-inch cubes
1 cup diced onion
1 cup corn kernels
One 4-ounce can roasted whole green chiles
½ cup chopped tomatillos
1 tablespoon olive oil
1 tablespoon minced garlic
1 tablespoon ground cumin
2 teaspoons paprika

2 teaspoons ground coriander
Kosher salt (if using table salt, decrease the amount by half;
   see page 16)
¼ teaspoon ground cinnamon
1 cup cooked long grain white rice, warm
½ cup chopped fresh cilantro
¼ cup sour cream
1 tablespoon fresh lime juice
Four 10- or 11-inch flour tortillas
Flavored tortilla suggestion: chipotle, salsa

Preheat oven to 400°F.

Combine the chicken, onion, corn, chiles, tomatillos, olive oil, garlic, cumin, paprika, coriander, 1 teaspoon kosher salt, and cinnamon in a large bowl. Mix well.

Spread the chicken mixture evenly into a 13-by-9-by-2-inch baking pan. Bake until chicken is cooked through, 10 to 15 minutes.

Add the rice, cilantro, sour cream, and lime juice; mix well. Season with kosher salt to taste. Divide among the tortillas and wrap (page 20).

Serves 4

tomatillos (A member of the tomato family, tomatillos look like small green tomatoes with a husk. They are a prominent ingredient in Mexican dishes, especially in salsas and sauces. They add a hint of acid to food and should be purchased when they are firm and blemish-free (take a peek under the husk when selecting them). Look for tomatillos in the produce department of supermarkets.)

german
engineering

You'll want to grab a stein of beer to drink with this wrap. This combination of potatoes, sausage, and mustard makes an ordinary day feel like Oktoberfest. If you're a mustard fan, dip this wrap in your favorite mustard to add an extra flavor dimension.

3 tablespoons sherry vinegar

2 tablespoons honey mustard

2 teaspoons caraway seeds

1½ teaspoons celery salt

Pepper

¼ cup plus 2 teaspoons olive oil

1 pound small red potatoes, cut into 1-inch cubes

Kosher salt (if using table salt, decrease the amount by half; see page 16)

1 cup diced onion

1 cup diced green bell pepper, seeds and ribs discarded

1 pound kielbasa sausage, cut in half lengthwise and sliced into ¼-inch half-circles

Four 10- or 11-inch flour tortillas

Combine the vinegar, mustard, caraway seeds, celery salt, and ¼ teaspoon pepper in a small bowl. Gradually whisk in ¼ cup of the olive oil. Set aside.

Place the potatoes in a large saucepan and cover with water. Add 1 tablespoon kosher salt and bring to a boil over high heat. Reduce heat and simmer until potatoes are tender when pierced with a fork, about 30 minutes. Remove from heat, drain and return the potatoes to the saucepan. Using a handheld masher or a large fork, mash into a coarse mixture. Add the vinegar mixture and mix well.

Heat the remaining 2 teaspoons olive oil in a large nonstick skillet over medium heat. Add the onion, bell pepper, ½ teaspoon kosher salt, and ¼ teaspoon pepper. Cook until onions and peppers become tender and start to brown, 5 to 7 minutes. Add the onions and peppers to the mashed potatoes and stir to combine. Wipe the skillet clean with a paper towel and return the skillet to the stove. Heat the skillet over high heat and add the kielbasa. Cook until brown, about 5 to 7 minutes. Add the potato mixture and mix well. Cook until warm. Divide among the tortillas and wrap (page 20).

Serves 4

hungry *hungarian*

This combination of onions, mushrooms, and beef gets its rich taste from the sour cream sauce. Mixed with egg noodles and wrapped in a tortilla, it is an unbeatable fusion of old and new.

¾ cup sour cream

3 tablespoons tomato paste

3 tablespoons ketchup

3 tablespoons chopped fresh parsley

1 tablespoon plus 2 teaspoons olive oil

2 cups sliced mushrooms

1 cup diced onion

Kosher salt (if using table salt, decrease the amount by half; see page 16)

Pepper

½ cup red wine

2 cups cooked egg noodles, warm

One 14-ounce can hearts of palm, drained and chopped

1 pound London broil, cut into ½-inch cubes

1 tablespoon paprika

Four 10- or 11-inch flour tortillas

Flavored tortilla suggestion: tomato

Combine the sour cream, tomato paste, ketchup, and parsley in a large bowl.

Heat 1 tablespoon of the olive oil in a large nonstick skillet over medium-high heat. Add the mushrooms, onion, ½ teaspoon kosher salt, and ¼ teaspoon pepper. Cook until the mushrooms begin to brown and the onion becomes tender, about 10 minutes. Add the wine and cook until the liquid is evaporated, about 5 minutes. Transfer to the sour cream mixture. Add the noodles and hearts of palm. Mix well.

Wipe the skillet clean with a paper towel and return the skillet to the stove. Add the remaining 2 teaspoons olive oil and heat over high heat. Add the London broil and season with ½ teaspoon kosher salt and the paprika. Cook until meat is brown on the outside but still pink in the center, about 5 minutes. Add the mushroom mixture. Cook on low heat until the mixture is warm, 1 to 2 minutes. Divide among the tortillas and wrap (page 20).

Serves 4

hearts of palm

HEARTS OF PALM are white, tender stems of the cabbage palm tree with a taste some compare to artichoke hearts. They are cultivated in tropical areas and can be found fresh in the areas where they are grown. You'll find hearts of palm in the canned vegetable section of supermarkets.

moroccan *missile*

This wrap pays homage to couscous, which is absolutely wonderful paired with this simple rendition of ratatouille.

⅓ cup tomato paste

¼ cup red wine vinegar

2 tablespoons olive oil

2 tablespoons chopped fresh thyme

1 tablespoon minced garlic

2 teaspoons herbes de Provence

3 cups diced eggplant (¾-inch cubes)

2 cups diced red bell pepper (¾-inch dice), seeds and
   ribs discarded

2 cups diced zucchini (¾-inch cubes)

1 cup diced onion (¾-inch dice)

Kosher salt (if using table salt, decrease the amount
   by half; see page 16)

Pepper

2 cups cooked couscous, warm

⅓ cup chopped fresh basil

1 cup goat cheese

Four 10- or 11-inch flour tortillas

Preheat oven to 400°F.

   Combine the tomato paste, vinegar, olive oil, thyme, garlic, and herbes de Provence in a large bowl. Add the eggplant, bell pepper, zucchini, and onion. Season with 1 teaspoon kosher salt and ½ teaspoon pepper. Toss to evenly coat vegetables.

   Spread the vegetable mixture into a 13-by-9-by-2-inch baking pan and bake until tender, about 45 minutes, stirring occasionally. Remove from oven. Add the couscous and basil. Season with kosher salt and pepper to taste.

   Divide the goat cheese among the tortillas and spread evenly over each tortilla, leaving at least a 1-inch border around the edge. Divide the vegetable mixture among the tortillas and wrap (page 20).

Serves 4

pizza pie

On the nights when Mary and Sara aren't cooking for a client, they can be found in front of the TV indulging in this ultra-scrumptious rendition of a calzone.

6 ounces pepperoni, diced

2 tablespoons olive oil

2 cups diced green bell pepper, seeds and ribs discarded

2 teaspoons minced garlic

Kosher salt (if using table salt, decrease the amount
  by half; see page 16)

Pepper

2 cups cooked long grain white rice, warm

1 cup marinara sauce

1 cup oil-packed sun-dried tomatoes, drained and chopped

¼ cup toasted pine nuts

1 tablespoon dried oregano

2 teaspoons balsamic vinegar

2 cups grated garlic jack cheese

Four 10- or 11-inch flour tortillas

Flavored tortilla suggestion: spinach, tomato

Preheat oven to 350°F. (See Note for microwave instructions.)

Heat a large nonstick skillet over medium-high heat. Add the pepperoni and cook until crispy, about 3 minutes. Transfer to a paper towel–lined plate to absorb the extra oil.

Wipe the skillet clean with a paper towel and return the skillet to the stove. Add the olive oil and heat over medium heat. Add the bell pepper and garlic. Season with ½ teaspoon kosher salt and ¼ teaspoon pepper and cook until tender, 5 to 7 minutes. Add the pepperoni, rice, marinara sauce, tomatoes, pine nuts, oregano, and vinegar.

Sprinkle the cheese evenly over the tortillas. Place the tortillas on a baking sheet and bake until cheese melts, about 2 minutes. Remove from the oven, divide the pepperoni mixture among the tortillas, and wrap (page 20).

N O T E : A microwave oven can be used instead of a conventional oven. Once tortillas have been prepared with the cheese, place tortillas, one at a time, on a paper towel–lined microwaveable plate. Cook on high power until the cheese melts, about 30 seconds.

Serves 4

marinara sauce
sun-dried tomatoes

(MARINARA SAUCE is a meatless tomato-based sauce. There are many varieties of ready-to-heat, high-quality sauces available. Our favorites are Newmans Own, Sutter Home, and Muir Glen. SUN-DRIED TOMATOES are tomatoes picked at the peak of their season and then dried in the sun or in a commercial oven. They have a concentrated, hearty flavor and are available in packages or oil-packed in jars and either in the produce department or near the tomato sauces in supermarkets. Oil-packed sun-dried tomatoes save time; just drain and use them. Other sun-dried tomatoes are easily reconstituted by simply covering with hot water until they are moist, about 10 minutes.)

porkie and bess

This dynamic mix of pork, white wine, herbs, olives, and capers was inspired by a recipe for Chicken Marbella in *The Silver Palate*. We prepare it with dried apricots which adds a fruit essence to this tangy vinegar mixture. Paired with couscous it becomes an elegant wrap perfect for a Saturday night dinner party.

¾ **cup white wine**

⅓ **cup red wine vinegar**

¼ **cup brown sugar**

¼ **cup minced garlic**

3 tablespoons plus 2 teaspoons olive oil

3 tablespoons dried oregano

2 teaspoons chopped fresh rosemary

Kosher salt (if using table salt, decrease the amount by half; see page 16)

½ **cup dried apricots, cut into quarters**

⅓ **cup Spanish green olives**

3 tablespoons capers, drained

1¼ **pounds boneless pork, cut into 1-inch cubes**

Pepper

2 cups cooked couscous, warm

Four 10- or 11-inch flour tortillas

Flavored tortilla suggestion: **whole wheat**

Combine the wine, vinegar, sugar, garlic, 3 tablespoons of the olive oil, oregano, rosemary, and 1 teaspoon kosher salt in a large nonreactive saucepan. Bring to a boil. Reduce heat, and add apricots, olives, and capers. Simmer until liquid is nearly evaporated, about 20 minutes. (A little bit of liquid ensures a moist final product; too much liquid will result in a soggy wrap.) Remove from heat.

Season the pork with 1 teaspoon kosher salt and pepper to taste. Heat the remaining 2 teaspoons olive oil in a large nonstick skillet over high heat. Add the pork and cook until browned on all sides, about 5 minutes. Add the wine mixture and couscous; stir to combine.

Divide the pork mixture among the tortillas and wrap (page 20).

Serves 4

shepherd's fare

This wrap was inspired by the English dish shepherd's pie, which was conceived for using leftover Sunday roast.

1 pound Yukon Gold (or small white) potatoes, peeled
  and cut into 1-inch cubes
Kosher salt (if using table salt, decrease the amount
  by half; see page 16)
½ cup goat cheese
½ cup whole milk
3 tablespoons olive oil
Pepper

1 pound ground lamb
1 tablespoon chopped fresh rosemary
1½ teaspoons ground fennel seeds
1½ teaspoons ground coriander
1 cup diced onion
2 cups packed chopped Swiss chard, tough stems removed
Four 10- or 11-inch flour tortillas
Flavored tortilla suggestion: spinach, tomato

Place the potatoes in a large saucepan and cover with water. Add 1 tablespoon kosher salt. Bring to a boil over high heat, then reduce heat and simmer, covered, until potatoes are tender when pierced with a fork, about 20 minutes. Drain the potatoes, return them to the pan, and mash, using a whisk or a large fork. Add the goat cheese, milk, and 1 tablespoon of the olive oil. Season with ½ teaspoon kosher salt and ¼ teaspoon pepper and set aside.

Heat a large nonstick skillet over high heat. Add the lamb, rosemary, fennel, and coriander. Cook until lamb is cooked through, 4 to 6 minutes. Transfer with a slotted spoon to a paper towel–lined plate and pat dry to remove extra oil.

Wipe the skillet clean with a paper towel and return the skillet to the stove. Add 1 tablespoon of the olive oil and heat over medium heat. Add the onion, ½ teaspoon kosher salt, and ¼ teaspoon pepper. Cook until onions are tender, about 5 minutes. Transfer to a medium bowl; add the lamb.

Return the skillet to the stove. Add the remaining 1 tablespoon olive oil and heat over medium heat. Add the Swiss chard and cook until wilted and tender, about 3 minutes. Add the lamb and onions. Keep warm over low heat.

Divide the mashed potatoes among the tortillas and spread evenly over each tortilla, leaving at least a 1-inch border around the edge. Divide the lamb mixture among the tortillas and wrap (page 20).

Serves 4

sweet

Yes, they drip, splash, and splatter. And no, they are not fat-free, calorie-free, or guilt-free. Even so, dessert is sometimes necessary. The *Ice Cream Wrapwich* will convert the staunchest of sugar cynics to a sweets fiend with one taste of the crumbled toffee, rich vanilla ice cream, and toothsome caramel sauce. The taste of a classic apple

ROCKY ROAD, THE WRAP
NECTAR SNAP
PLUM DECADENT
ICE CREAM WRAPWICH
BANANA BETTY
ABBA ZABBA
APPLE WRAPOVER

t o o t h

turnover is within easy reach in *Apple Wrapover*. Pies, crumbles,

and crisps will soon be tossed aside after one bite of *Nectar Snap*,

which is made with nectarines and gingersnaps.

gratification

rocky road, *the wrap*

During the Depression, when Dreyer's Grand Ice Cream created Rocky Road to reflect the times, it turned the ice cream industry on its ear. This wrap does the same for beloved chocolate desserts. Warning: Do not consume without a tall glass of cold milk.

1 cup semisweet chocolate morsels (not milk chocolate)

2 tablespoons butter

2 tablespoons light corn syrup

¾ cup Rice Krispies

½ cup firmly packed miniature marshmallows

½ cup chopped toasted pecans

Four 8-inch flour tortillas

Flavored tortilla suggestion: cocoa

Fill the bottom of a double boiler with 1 to 2 inches of water. Bring to a boil over high heat. Remove from heat. Combine the chocolate, butter, and corn syrup in the top of the double boiler set over the hot water. Stir with a plastic spatula until the chocolate and butter are completely melted. (Be sure that all utensils are dry before using or the chocolate will seize.) Add the remaining ingredients. Mix well. Divide among the tortillas and wrap (page 20).

Serves 4

nectar *snap*

This is a great dessert for entertaining because it can be made ahead of time and then set in the oven to warm when dinner begins. Just as guests are finishing the main course, this delectable treat can be pulled out of the oven.

2½ cups firmly packed peeled, pitted, and diced
   nectarines (1-inch dice)
2 tablespoons honey
2 teaspoons cornstarch
Kosher salt

1 tablespoon butter
1 cup firmly packed chopped gingersnaps
Four 8-inch flour tortillas
Flavored tortilla suggestion: cinnamon spice, peach

Combine the nectarines, honey, cornstarch, and a pinch of kosher salt in a medium bowl.

Melt the butter in a large nonstick skillet over low heat. Increase the heat to high and add the nectarine mixture. Cook until nectarines are soft, 1 to 2 minutes. Remove from heat.

Fold in the gingersnaps and let sit 15 minutes. Divide among the tortillas and wrap (page 20).

FOR A BAKED VERSION: Preheat oven to 375°F. Line a baking sheet with aluminum foil and place wraps seam side down on baking sheet. Brush with 1 tablespoon melted butter and sprinkle with 2 teaspoons sugar. Bake until crust is crispy, about 30 minutes. Be certain there are no holes or tears in the tortilla before baking or all of the juices will escape, leaving you with a messy cluster of dried fruit.

Serves 4

plum *decadent*

Plums are at their peak of perfection in summer—less sweet and more subtle—making this recipe good year-round. Use firm, ripe plums for the best results.

½ cup apple juice

3 tablespoons instant tapioca

2½ cups thinly sliced plums (¼-inch-thick slices)

⅓ cup sugar

1 teaspoon almond extract

¼ teaspoon allspice

Kosher salt

2 tablespoons butter

Four 8-inch flour tortillas

Flavored tortilla suggestion: cinnamon spice, peach

Combine the apple juice and tapioca in a small bowl and let sit at least 10 minutes.

Combine the plums, sugar, almond extract, allspice, and a pinch of kosher salt in a large bowl. Stir in the apple juice/tapioca mixture. Melt the butter in a large nonstick skillet over low heat. Increase the heat to high and add the plums. Cook until plums are soft and liquid is nearly evaporated, 6 to 8 minutes, stirring occasionally. Remove from heat and cool to room temperature. Divide mixture among the tortillas and wrap (page 20).

FOR A BAKED VERSION: Preheat oven to 375°F. Line a baking sheet with aluminum foil and place wraps seam side down on baking sheet. Brush with 1 tablespoon melted butter and sprinkle with 2 teaspoons sugar. Bake until crust is crispy, about 30 minutes. Be certain there are no holes or tears in the tortilla before baking or all of the juices will escape, leaving you with a messy cluster of dried fruit.

Serves 4

ice cream
wrapwich

This wrap is delicious when it is first made, but it is even better when it is put in the freezer for an hour or so before serving. While in the freezer the tortilla absorbs moisture from the caramel sauce and ice cream, making it all the more luscious. For a fun presentation, roll this wrap into a cone shape.

¼ **cup cajeta or caramel sauce**
2 **cups vanilla Swiss almond ice cream**
½ **cup chopped toffee**

Four 8-inch flour tortillas
Flavored tortilla suggestion: **cocoa**

Divide the cajeta sauce among the tortillas and spread evenly over each tortilla, leaving at least a 1-inch border around the edge. Sprinkle with the toffee. Divide the ice cream among the tortillas and wrap (page 20).

Serves 4

cajeta

CAJETA is a rich caramel sauce imported from Mexico. It is made with goat's milk and is traditionally used as a filling in crepes with sliced apples and caramelized nuts or is mixed with mild cheeses. If you can find cajeta in your supermarket or a market that carries Hispanic food, we strongly recommend it; otherwise, use caramel sauce. One caramel sauce that we like is Lesley B. Fay's French Vanilla Caramel.

banana betty

Bananas have long held the hearts of dessert lovers, from bananas Foster to banana cream pie. This lush dessert bridges the gap between a crumble and a pie.

6 tablespoons unsalted butter
¼ cup firmly packed light brown sugar
¼ cup plus 2 tablespoons all-purpose flour
¼ cup chopped hazelnuts
Kosher salt
⅓ cup granulated sugar

1 tablespoon fresh lime juice
2 cups firmly packed sliced bananas
1 tablespoon hazelnut liqueur
Four 8-inch flour tortillas
Flavored tortilla suggestion: **cinnamon spice**

Preheat the oven to 350°F.

Melt the 2 tablespoons butter in a small saucepan over low heat. Add the brown sugar and stir to dissolve. Remove from heat. Add the flour, nuts, and a pinch of kosher salt. Spread on a baking sheet and bake until golden brown and crispy, 12 to 15 minutes. Let cool.

Combine the remaining 4 tablespoons butter, the granulated sugar, lime juice, and a pinch of kosher salt in a large nonstick skillet. Heat over low heat until butter melts, about 1 minute. Increase heat and cook until the mixture begins to brown, about 3 minutes. Add the bananas and liqueur. Cook until bananas are coated, about 1 minute. Transfer to a bowl.

Chop the crumb topping and add to the banana mixture. Stir to combine. Divide among the tortillas and wrap (page 20). Enjoy this wrap immediately.

FOR A BAKED VERSION: Preheat oven to 375°F. Line a baking sheet with aluminum foil and place wraps seam side down on baking sheet. Brush with 1 tablespoon melted butter and sprinkle with 2 teaspoons sugar. Bake until crust is crispy, about 30 minutes. Be certain there are no holes or tears in the tortilla before baking or all of the juices will escape, leaving you with a messy cluster of dried fruit.

Serves 4

abba zabba

Pay no mind to the odd assortment of ingredients in this dessert wrap. The combination of peanut butter, white chocolate, salted peanuts, and pretzels will wow you.

¾ **cup cream cheese, softened**

⅓ **cup peanut butter**

3 **tablespoons powdered sugar**

1 **cup chopped yogurt-covered pretzels**

⅓ **cup white chocolate chips**

⅓ **cup salted peanuts**

Four 8-inch flour tortillas

Combine the cream cheese and peanut butter in a medium bowl. Mix thoroughly. Stir in the powdered sugar until thoroughly combined. Add the remaining ingredients and mix well. Divide among the tortillas and wrap (page 20). Eat immediately, or refrigerate for up to 1 hour before serving.

Serves 4

apple
wrapover

Bake this wrap in the oven, top it with a slice of Cheddar cheese or a scoop of vanilla ice cream, and you have reinvented Americana.

¼ cup maple syrup
2 tablespoons dark rum
2 tablespoons butter
1 teaspoon fresh lemon juice
1 teaspoon ground cinnamon

Kosher salt
4 cups peeled, cored, and diced apples (½-inch dice)
⅓ cup crème fraîche
Four 8-inch flour tortillas
Flavored tortilla suggestion: cinnamon spice

Combine the syrup, rum, butter, lemon juice, cinnamon, and a pinch of kosher salt in a large nonstick skillet. Heat over high heat until mixture begins to bubble. Add the apples and cook until tender, about 10 minutes. Add the crème fraîche and cook until liquid is thick, about 2 minutes. Divide the filling among the tortillas and wrap (page 20).

FOR A BAKED VERSION: Preheat oven to 375°F. Line a baking sheet with aluminum foil and place wraps seam side down on baking sheet. Brush with 1 tablespoon melted butter and sprinkle with 2 teaspoons sugar. Bake until crust is crispy, about 30 minutes. Be certain there are no holes or tears in the tortilla before baking or all of the juices will escape, leaving you with a messy cluster of dried fruit.

Serves 4

crème fraîche

(CRÈME FRAÎCHE, a thick cream that has a taste similar to sour cream, is ideal for cooking and garnishing because it is less tart and will not curdle when heated. Commercial brands are widely available. It can also be made at home by simply combining equal amounts of sour cream and heavy cream in a nonreactive bowl. Let the mixture sit at room temperature for 8 to 24 hours, until thick. Refrigerate unused portions for up to one week.)

The following companies offer mail-order service for products that may be hard to find. Most can direct you to stores in your area where their brands are available.

indian ingredients

MEZBAN
2690 SLOUGH STREET
MISSISSAUGA, ONTARIO L4T 1G3
CANADA
905.673.7728
VINDALOO SAUCE

mexican ingredients

ANDRE PROST, INC.
OLD SAYBROOK, CT 06475
800.243.0897
HOT ADOBO MARINADE

FLAPPERS
MEXICAN FOOD PRODUCTS COMPANY
1555 GALVEZ AVENUE
SAN FRANCISCO, CA 94124
415.648.8550
SWEET AND SAVORY FLAVORED TORTILLAS

MATTHEWS MUSTARD COMPANY
1340 INDUSTRIAL AVENUE
PETALUMA, CA 94952
800.894.MATT (IN CALIFORNIA)
707.762.5762 (OUTSIDE CALIFORNIA)
FLAVORED TORTILLAS

miscellaneous

LESLEY B. FAY INC.

P.O. BOX 2054

SONOMA, CA 94576

707.996.2600

CARAMEL SAUCE

CHUKAR CHERRY COMPANY

320 WINE COUNTRY ROAD

PROSSER, WA 99350

800.624.9544

WWW.TELEVAR.COM/CHUKAR

DRIED CHERRIES

WILLIAMS-SONOMA

100 NORTHPOINT STREET

SAN FRANCISCO, CA 94133

800.541.2233

HERBES DE PROVENCE,

PRESERVED AND DRIED LEMONGRASS,

PURE CITRUS OILS

pan-asian ingredients

THAI KITCHENS

EPICUREAN INTERNATIONAL, INC.

P.O. BOX 13242

BERKELEY, CA 94701

800.967.8424

CURRY PASTES,

LEMONGRASS

SAVEUR SPECIALTY FOODS

13158 STEWART COURT

SARATOGA, CA 95070

408.867.2289

SAVEUR@BEST.COM

PEANUT SAUCE

SUSHI CHEF

BAYCLIFF COMPANY, INC.

242 EAST 72ND STREET

NEW YORK, NY 10021

212.772.6078

WASABI, RICE WINE VINEGAR,

PICKLED GINGER, NORI,

SHORT GRAIN RICE, AND MORE

index

table of equivalents

The exact equivalents in the following tables have been rounded for convenience.

liquid and dry measures

U.S.	METRIC
¼ teaspoon	1.25 milliliters
½ teaspoon	2.5 milliliters
1 teaspoon	5 milliliters
1 tablespoon (3 teaspoons)	15 milliliters
1 fluid ounce (2 tablespoons)	30 milliliters
¼ cup	60 milliliters
⅓ cup	80 milliliters
1 cup	120 milliliters
1 pint (2 cups)	480 milliliters
1 quart (4 cups, 32 ounces)	960 milliliters
1 gallon (4 quarts)	3.84 liters
1 ounce (by weight)	28 grams
¼ pound (4 ounces)	114 grams
1 pound	454 grams
2.2 pounds	1 kilogram

length measures

U.S.	METRIC
⅛ inch	3 millimeters
¼ inch	6 millimeters
½ inch	12 millimeters
1 in	2.5 centimeters

oven temperatures

FAHRENHEIT	CELSIUS	GAS
250	120	½
275	140	1
300	150	2
325	160	3
350	180	4
375	190	5
400	200	6
425	220	7
450	230	8
475	240	9
500	260	10